Skills Practice
Annotated Teacher's Edition

Level 5
Book 2

SRA

Columbus, OH

SRAonline.com

 SRA

Send all inquiries to this address:
SRA/McGraw-Hill
4400 Easton Commons
Columbus, OH 43219-6188

ISBN: 978-0-07-610497-0
MHID: 0-07-610497-4

2 3 4 5 6 7 8 9 QPD 13 12 11 10 09 08

The McGraw-Hill Companies

Table of Contents

Unit 4 Our Corner of the Universe

5 Unit Going West

Unit 6 Call of Duty

Name _____ **Date** _____

Words with Greek Roots

**Focus** **Greek roots** are common in the English language. Identifying and understanding Greek roots can help you define difficult words. When you know the meaning of a root, you can figure out the meanings of many words that contain that root.

Practice **Think of a word that uses each Greek root given below. Write the word on the line, and then use it in a sentence.**

1. *tele* means "far away" **Possible Answer** television

Possible Answer After I finish my homework, I watch television before going to bed.

2. *tri* means "three" **Possible Answer** tricycle

Possible Answer My little sister rides a tricycle.

3. *aqua* means "water" **Possible Answer** aquarium

Possible Answer There are many exotic fish in the aquarium.

4. *bio* means "life" **Possible Answer** biography

Possible Answer I read a biography of Walt Disney last year.

Apply Each group of words below uses the same Greek root. The roots' meanings are listed in the box. Use your knowledge of words to select the correct meaning, and write it on the line.

| measure | eye | star | sound | study | water |

5. phonograph, telephone, phonics, xylophone

   phon means _____ sound _____

6. hydrant, dehydrated, hydroelectric

   hydro means _____ water _____

7. centimeter, speedometer, thermometer

   meter means _____ measure _____

8. asteroid, astronomy, astronaut

   aster means _____ star _____

9. biology, psychology, geology, physiology

   ology means _____ study _____

10. optical, Cyclops, optician, optometrist

    ops means _____ eye _____

Name _____ Date _____

Selection Vocabulary

Focus

infinity (in•fin'•i•tē) *n.* the condition of having no limits (page 354)

disks (disks) *n.* plural of **disk:** a flat, thin, round object (page 356)

clusters (klus'•tərz) *n.* plural of **cluster:** a number of things of the same kind that are grouped together (page 357)

bulges (bəl'•jez) *n.* plural of **bulge:** a rounded part that swells out (page 357)

cosmic (koz'•mik) *adj.* of or relating to the universe (page 358)

spokes (spōks) *n.* plural of **spoke:** one of the rods or bars that connect the rim of a wheel to the hub (page 358)

galaxy (gal'•ək•sē) *n.* a very large group of stars (page 359)

spiral (spī'•rəl) *n.* a curve that keeps winding. A spiral may wind inward and outward or downward and upward (page 359)

collapse (kə•laps') *v.* to fall in; break down (page 361)

detect (di•tekt') *v.* to find out or notice; discover (page 360)

Practice **Circle the word that correctly completes each sentence.**

1. The spider crawled round and round in a _____ shape to spin its web.
   a. cosmic **(b.)** spiral **c.** bulges

2. Terrell's house of cards began to _____ when he sneezed.
   (a.) collapse **b.** detect **c.** spiral

3. _____ of diamonds hung from the princess's ears.
   a. bulges **b.** spokes **(c.)** clusters

4. I did not _____ any hints about the surprise party.
   a. spiral **(b.)** detect **c.** collapse

5. Numbers increase to _____ because they never end.
   a. galaxy   **b.** cosmic   **c.** infinity

6. A _____ may contain billions of stars.
   a. galaxy   **b.** spiral   **c.** cosmic

7. The _____ of the bicycle wheel were broken when he hit the curb.
   a. spokes   **b.** clusters   **c.** bulges

8. After long missions, scientists were unsure of the effects of _____ rays on astronauts.
   a. bulges   **b.** spiral   **c.** cosmic

9. The large _____ of the apparatus kept spinning.
   a. disks   **b.** infinity   **c.** detect

10. The _____ of the large balloon were almost ready to burst from all of the air.
   a. cosmic   **b.** bulges   **c.** spiral

Apply   Match each word to its definition on the right.

11. galaxy   **a.** rounded parts that swell out

12. clusters   **b.** to find out or notice

13. collapse   **c.** things of the same kind that are grouped together

14. disks   **d.** to fall in, break down

15. bulges   **e.** a very large group of stars

16. detect   **f.** flat, thin, round objects

Name _____ Date _____

Classify and Categorize

Focus Classifying and categorizing are ways of organizing information. They can help you better understand and remember what you read.

- **Classifying** is identifying the similarities that objects, characters, or events have in common with each other, and then grouping them by their similarities.

- **Categorizing** is the act of organizing the objects, characters, or events into groups, or categories.

Practice Look at the first page of "The Universe" and list five classifications found in the address.

1. name
2. street
3. planet
4. solar system
5. galaxy

Apply On the diagram below, heavenly bodies are categorized as stars, planets, and nebulas. Complete the diagram by thinking of things that could be classified under the headings *Stars*, *Planets*, or *Nebulas*.

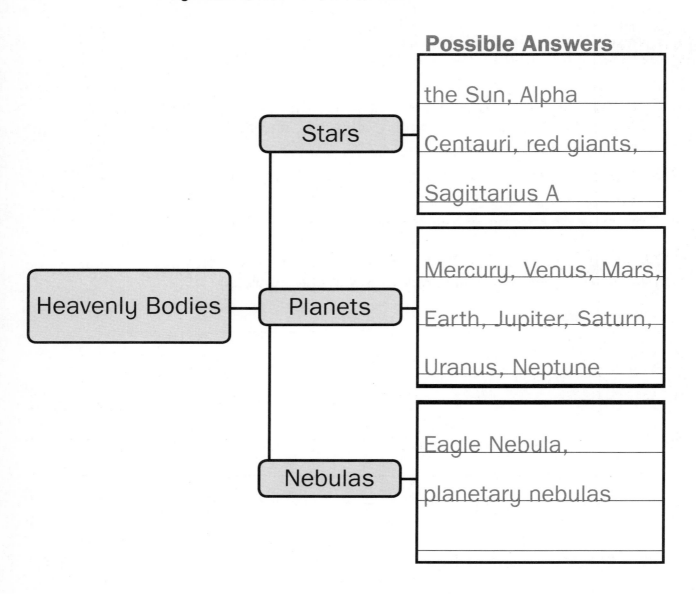

Possible Answers

Stars
the Sun, Alpha Centauri, red giants, Sagittarius A

Heavenly Bodies

Planets
Mercury, Venus, Mars, Earth, Jupiter, Saturn, Uranus, Neptune

Nebulas
Eagle Nebula, planetary nebulas

Name _____ **Date** _____

Recording Concept Information

As I read the selection, this is what I added to my understanding of Our Corner of the Universe.

- "The Universe" by Seymour Simon

  Possible Answer I learned that our corner of the universe is quite small compared to the vastness of space.

  _____

- "Circles, Squares, and Daggers: How Native Americans Watched the Skies" by Elsa Marston

  Possible Answer I learned that ancient civilizations were also fascinated by astronomy. People from every time period have looked to the stars for answers.

- "The Mystery of Mars" by Sally Ride and Tam O'Shaugnessy

  Possible Answer I learned that not all planets can support life.

  _____

- "Apollo 11: First Moon Landing" by Michael D. Cole

  Possible Answer I learned about the significance of the accomplishment of landing on the moon and its effects on the world.

- "Ellen Ochoa: Reaching for the Stars" by Claire Daniel

  Possible Answer I learned that being an astronaut requires a lot of hard work, dedication, and studying. Ellen Ochoa opened the door for many people to become astronauts.

Name _____ **Date** _____

Knowledge about Our Corner of the Universe

- This is what I know about our corner of the universe
  before reading the unit.

  Possible Answer There is less gravity in space. Astronauts
  walked on the moon and in space.

  _____

  _____

  _____

  _____

- These are some things about our corner of the universe
  that I would like to talk about and understand better.

  Possible Answer What are black holes? How big is space?
  Will I ever be able to travel to space? How many stars are
  there?

  _____

  _____

  _____

Reminder: I should read this page again when I get to
the end of the unit to see how much my ideas about our
corner of the universe have changed.

Name _____ **Date** _____

Ideas about *Our Corner of the Universe*

Of the ideas discussed in class about *Our Corner of the Universe*, these are the ones I found most interesting.

Possible Answer Why did past civilizations practice astonomy?

_____

_____

_____

_____

_____

_____

_____

_____

_____

_____

_____

_____

_____

_____

_____

_____

_____

Ideas about *Our Corner of the Universe* (continued)

Write down the ideas you found most interesting about the selection "The Universe." Discuss your ideas with the class.

Possible Answer The universe is larger than anything we can comprehend. We will most likely never know just what may be all around us.

Name _____ **Date** _____

Letter of Request

Think

Audience: Who will read your letter of request?

<u>**Possible Answer** scientists at NASA</u>

Purpose: Why are you writing a letter of request?
<u>**Possible Answer** I want to know when the</u>
<u>International Space Station will be complete.</u>

Prewriting

A letter of request is a type of business letter. Use the lines below to plan your request.

○ • Where will the letter be sent? <u>**Possible Answer** NASA</u>
<u>Headquarters, Suite 1M32, Washington,</u>
<u>DC 20546-0001</u>

• What will your salutation be? <u>**Possible Answer** Dear NASA:</u>
_____

• What information are you requesting and why? <u>**Possible Answer**</u>
<u>I want to know when the International Space Station will</u>
<u>be finished. I want to be an astronaut and would like to</u>
<u>work there.</u>

○ • How do you want the reader to respond to your request? <u>**Possible**</u>
<u>**Answer** NASA can send a letter back to me.</u>

Now on a separate sheet of paper, put the information above into the form of a business letter.

Revising

Use this checklist to revise your letter of request.

☐ Did you put the date, your name, and your address in the top left corner?

☐ Is your request stated clearly in the first sentence?

☐ Did you explain why you want the information?

☐ Did you thank the reader for his or her help?

☐ Is your letter polite and businesslike?

Editing/Proofreading

Use this checklist to correct mistakes.

☐ Did you follow the correct format for a business letter?

☐ Did you check for spelling errors?

☐ Did you capitalize the correct words?

☐ Did you indent the paragraphs? Remember that a business letter's paragraphs are not indented.

Publishing

Use this checklist to get your letter ready to mail.

☐ Type your letter on a computer and print it. You may use the automatic business letter tool if you use a computer.

☐ Reread your letter for errors.

☐ Sign your letter.

☐ Address and proofread the envelope.

☐ Place the letter in the envelope.

☐ Put the correct postage on the envelope and mail it.

Name _____ Date _____

Spelling

Focus
- **Irregular plurals** do not follow the regular rules for forming plurals. They do not end in *-s* or *-es*. Sometimes the base word spelling changes to form the plural, and sometimes it does not change at all:
child, children; salmon, salmon; person, people

- Understanding and identifying **Greek roots** and their meanings can help you define and spell difficult and unfamiliar words. Here are some of the Greek roots in the spelling words and their meanings:
cycl = "circle" or "ring"; ***onym*** = "name"; ***astr*** and ***aster*** = "star"

Word List
1. asterisk
2. antonym
3. cycle
4. phenomena
5. alumnus
6. cyclone
7. radius
8. astronomy
9. index
10. phenomenon
11. bicycle
12. indices
13. alumni
14. synonym
15. stimulus
16. radii
17. disaster
18. asteroid
19. stimuli
20. astronaut

Practice **Each of the following examples includes at least one Greek root.**
Write the spelling word represented in each line.

1. bi + cycl + e =   bicycle
2. aster + isk =   asterisk
3. dis + aster =   disaster
4. cycl + one =   cyclone
5. syn + onym =   synonym
6. aster + oid =   asteroid
7. cycl + e =   cycle
8. astr + onomy =   astronomy
9. ant + onym =   antonym
10. astr + onaut =   astronaut

On the lines, write the singular and plural form of the spelling words that begin with the following prefixes.

stimu-

11. singular: stimulus

12. plural: stimuli

16. plural: indices

alum-

17. singular: alumnus

18. plural: alumni

phenome-

13. singular: phenomenon

14. plural: phenomena

rad-

19. singular: radius

20. plural: radii

ind-

15. singular: index

 **Apply** If the underlined noun in the sentence is incorrect, write the correct form from the spelling list on the line. If it is correct, write *correct.*

21. Too many <u>stimuluses</u> make it hard to study.

stimuli

22. That book has two <u>indixes</u>.

indices

23. A thunderstorm is a natural <u>phenomena</u>.

phenomenon

24. My father and mother are both <u>alumni</u> of Harding High.

correct

25. A fiction book usually does not have an <u>indices</u>.

index

26. The larger the circle, the longer its <u>radius</u>.

correct

27. Those two players are <u>phenomenas</u>!

phenomena

28. Her uncle is an <u>alumnu</u> of a state college.

alumnus

29. The pay raise was a <u>stimuli</u> for them to work harder.

stimulus

30. All <u>radii</u> in a circle are the same length.

correct

Name _____ **Date** _____

Demonstrative Pronouns and Hyphens

Focus

A **demonstrative pronoun** demonstrates by indicating or pointing out something. *This*, *these*, *that*, and *those* are demonstrative pronouns.

- To refer to things that are nearby, use *this*, singular, or *these*, plural.

- To refer to things that are far away, use *that*, singular, or *those*, plural.

- **This** is the shirt I will wear. Are **these** the papers you needed?

- **That** is the best idea so far. Where are you putting **those?**

Hyphens are used in the following cases:

- to divide a word between syllables when you run out of space on a line

- for some compound nouns

  good-bye   *teeter-totter*   *sister-in-law*

- when forming a compound modifier, such as an adjective formed from two words written in front of a noun

  second-place finish   *orange-red sun*   *Chicago-style pizza*

- for numbers and fractions that are written out

  ninety-nine   *forty-six*   *one-fourth*

Practice

Use the clue in parentheses to choose a demonstrative pronoun that will correctly complete each sentence. Also, place hyphens where they are missing.

1. ____That, first-place____ was Samantha's last chance to reach first place. (far away)

2. ____This, one-fourth____ recipe uses one fourth cup of sugar. (nearby)

3. How will Uncle Reuben know if ____those, Chicago-style____ pizza slices are Chicago style? (far away)

4. Give me a hand with ____these, ice-cube____ ice cube trays before the ice melts. (nearby)

Apply   ***This, these, that,*** **and** ***those*** **are not always pronouns. They are adjectives when they modify nouns, as in** ***this house*** **or** ***those people.*** **In each sentence, determine whether** ***this, these, that,*** **or** ***those*** **is used as a pronoun or an adjective. Write** ***P*** **for pronoun or** ***A*** **for adjective. Also, place hyphens where they are missing.**

5. Do you remember Nagid, **that** boy who moved to

   Dallas Fort Worth last year? _A, Dallas-Fort Worth_

6. We do not know who put **this** here, but it needs to move

   one-half inch to the left. _____P_____

7. I pulled **these** closer so I could reach them with my

   salad fork. _____P_____

8. What are **those** things on Brijesh's swing set?

   _____A_____

9. Could you tell her **that** shirt isn't blue green?

   _____A, blue-green_____

10. I need help with **those** twenty two math questions.

    _____A, twenty-two_____

11. Would you give **this** to my brother in law?

    _____P, brother-in-law_____

12. Rubber bands should hold **these** together.

    _____P_____

Name _____ **Date** _____

Multiple-Meaning Words and Suffix *-tion/-ion*

Focus

Multiple-meaning words are words that have more than one meaning, but the same origin. You will often need to look at context clues to figure out which meaning is being used in a particular sentence.

The suffix **-tion/-ion** is used to turn words into nouns.

> compose (verb) + *-tion* = composition
>
> propose (verb) + *-tion* = proposition

Practice

Add the suffix to the following words. Write the word on the line and provide at least two meanings for the resulting multiple-meaning word.

1. apply

application _____

Possible Answers formal request for something; spreading liquid on a surface

2. reserve

reservation _____

Possible Answers arrangement made beforehand; land set aside _____

3. inflate

inflation _____

Possible Answers act of filling with air; the general rise in consumer prices over time

Apply Add the suffix *-tion/-ion* to each word below to create a multiple-meaning word. On the lines provided, use the resulting word in two sentences. Each sentence should reflect a different meaning.

4. project <u>projection</u>

Possible Answer <u>Our business fell short of the year's projections.</u>

Possible Answer <u>The projection seemed so real, but it was only a movie.</u>

5. form <u>formation</u>

Possible Answer <u>The rock formation in the mountains was created thousands</u>

<u>of years ago.</u>

Possible Answer <u>My parents love to watch my nephew march in formation</u>
with the band.

6. direct <u>direction</u>

Possible Answer <u>Even with his directions to the party, we got lost.</u>

Possible Answer <u>The direction of the company changed when the new president</u>

<u>took over.</u>

7. deposit <u>deposition</u>

Possible Answer <u>The witness gave his deposition to the attorney.</u>

Possible Answer <u>Over the years, there has been a great deal of deposition of</u>

<u>soil near the mouth of the river.</u>

8. operate <u>operation</u>

Possible Answer <u>The doctor told us that the operation went well.</u>

Possible Answer <u>The abandoned power plant is no longer in operation.</u>

Name _____ Date _____

Selection Vocabulary

Focus

stargazers (stär'•gā•zerz) *n.* plural of **stargazer:** a person who studies the stars (page 370)

observatories (əb•zûr•və•to r•ēz) *n.* plural of **observatory:** a place with telescopes for observing the sun, moon, planets, and stars (page 370)

archaeology (är'•kē•ol'•ə•jē) *n.* the study of the way humans lived long ago. Archaeologists dig up the remains of ancient cities and towns and then study the tools, weapons, pottery, and other things they find. (page 370)

abandoned (ə•ban'•dənd) *v.* past tense of **abandon:** to leave and not return (page 370)

devised (di•vīzd') *v.* past tense of **devise:** to think out, invent, or plan (page 370)

dramatic (drə•ma'•tik) *adj.* exciting or interesting (page 371)

calculations (kal'•kyə•lā' •shənz) *n.* plural of **calculation:** the result of counting, computing, or figuring (page 373)

vertical (vûr'•ti•kəl) *adj.* straight up and down (page 375)

bull's-eye (boolz•ī') *n.* the center of a circle or target (page 377)

solar (sō'•lər) *adj.* having to do with or coming from the sun (page 378)

Practice Write *T* in the blank if the sentence for the vocabulary word is correct. Write *F* if the sentence is false. For every *F* answer, write the vocabulary word that fits the definition.

1. *Stargazers* are places to study the stars. <u>F,</u> <u>Observatories</u>

2. The center of a circle or target is a *bull's-eye.* <u>T</u> _____

3. Something *vertical* is exciting or interesting. <u>F,</u> <u>dramatic</u>

4. *Calculations* are the result of counting, computing, or figuring.

_T_

5. A project that has been *devised* has been thought out, invented, or planned. _T_

6. *Solar* means "coming from the sun."

_T_

7. A person who *abandoned* his or her home left and did not return.

_T_

8. *Archaeology* is the study of the life and culture of people

of the past. _T_

9. *Observatories* are people who study the stars.

_F,_ _Stargazers_

Apply **Review the vocabulary words and definitions from "Circles, Squares, and Daggers: How Native Americans Watched the Skies." Write two sentences that each use at least one of the vocabulary words from this lesson.**

10. **Possible Answer** Stargazers use telescopes in observatories to study the stars.

11. **Possible Answer** My aunt studied archaeology in college and now travels all over the world.

Name _____ **Date** _____

Compare and Contrast

> **Focus** Writers compare and contrast to paint a clearer picture of the people and things they are writing about.
>
> - To **compare** means to tell how things, ideas, events, or characters are alike.
> - To **contrast** means to tell how things, ideas, events, or characters are different.

Practice The author of "Circles, Squares, and Daggers" describes how ancient Native Americans observed the sky. On the lines below, compare and contrast two things each about the Bighorn Medicine Wheel observatory and the observatories used by the Anasazi.

Compare

1. **Possible Answer** The Bighorn Medicine Wheel and the Anasazi sun dagger are both built from rock. They both track the sun's movement during the year.

_____

Contrast

2. **Possible Answer** The Anasazi sun dagger marks only the equinoxes and solstice. The Medicine Wheel shows the alignments of stars and planets as well. The Medicine Wheel is built out in the open, but the Anasazi sun rooms are enclosed.

Apply   Read each sentence and tell whether it shows a comparison or a contrast. Then, rewrite each sentence to reflect the other term, either compare or contrast. Note the change that occurs in the meaning.

3. Dave and Ed both finished all their vegetables. ___comparison___

Dave finished his vegetables, but Ed did not.

4. Martha plays the trombone, while Janet plays the cello. ___contrast___

Both Martha and Janet play the cello.

5. I like to read mysteries just like my sister Gina. ___comparison___

Unlike my sister Gina, I like to read mysteries.

6. Both cats and dogs make good pets. ___comparison___

Cats make good pets, but dogs are hard to care for.

7. Jacob and Jason are twins, but Jacob is slightly taller. ___contrast___

Jacob and Jason are identical twins.

Name _____ **Date** _____

Formulating Questions and Problems

A good question or problem to investigate:

Possible Answer Why do we practice astronomy? _____

_____

_____

_____

_____

Why this is an interesting question or problem:

Possible Answer It allows me to compare my civilization's

beliefs with those of past civilizations. _____

_____

_____

_____

Some other things I wonder about this question
or problem:

Possible Answers Will we ever accomplish the goal of

colonizing the Moon or other planets? What are the benefits?

What are the drawbacks? _____

_____

_____

Formulating Questions and Problems (continued)

My investigation group's question or problem:

Possible Answer Is it possible that there could be life on other planets?

_____

_____

_____

What our investigation will contribute to the rest of the class:

Possible Answer Our answers and questions will contribute to the greater class discussion of the topic.

_____

_____

_____

Some other things I wonder about this question or problem:

Possible Answers If there is life on other planets, is it intelligent life?

_____

_____

_____

Inquiry • _Skills Practice 2_

Name _____ **Date** _____

Book Review

Think

Audience: Who will read your book review?

<u>**Possible Answer** a friend</u>

Purpose: What do you want your book review to do?

<u>**Possible Answer** I want to convince other people to read</u>
this story.

Prewriting **Use the organizer below to plan your book review.**

Title: <u>**Possible Answer** *Harriet the Spy* by Louise Fitzhugh</u>

Author's Purpose: <u>**Possible Answer** to entertain</u>

Summary: <u>**Possible Answer** Harriet spies on people in her</u>

<u>neighborhood. She keeps notes in a secret notebook. Her</u>

<u>friends read the notebook, and they become angry. Harriet</u>

<u>learns to use her skills as a reporter for the student paper.</u>

Your Opinions: <u>**Possible Answer** Harriet was a likeable and</u>

<u>believable character. The author did a good job of showing</u>

<u>how Harriet became a better person.</u>

Your Recommendation: <u>**Possible Answer** I loved the book and</u>

<u>would recommend it to anyone.</u>

Revising
Use this checklist to revise your book review.

☐ Did you use formal language in your writing?

☐ Did you use a thesaurus to choose precise and vivid words?

☐ Are your opinions explained with examples?

☐ Will your ideas convince others to read or not read the story?

Editing/Proofreading
Use this checklist to correct mistakes.

☐ Did you spell the title and author's name correctly?

☐ Did you check all capitalization and punctuation, including hyphens?

☐ Did you check your spelling of possessive nouns?

☐ Have you correctly used demonstrative pronouns?

Publishing
Use this checklist to prepare for publication.

☐ Write neatly or type on a computer to create a final copy. Be sure to use the correct formatting.

☐ Provide illustrations for your review or a photograph of the author.

Name _____ **Date** _____

Spelling

Focus

Nouns are formed when the suffix *-tion/-ion* is added to a base or root word. If a word already ends in *t,* then simply add *-ion*. If a word ends in *e,* drop the *e* before adding the ending. Finally, in some cases, the base word changes in spelling before the *-tion/-ion* ending is added, as in *attend, attention.*

Word List

1. construction
2. subtraction
3. intersection
4. attention
5. institution
6. retribution
7. obstruction
8. contradiction
9. retraction
10. abolition
11. suggestions
12. instruction
13. contribution
14. revolution
15. selection
16. detection
17. pollution
18. reflection
19. retention
20. deflection

Practice

On the lines, write the spelling words that are formed from the following base words and suffixes.

1. pollute + ion = __pollution__
2. suggest + ion + s = __suggestions__
3. abolish + tion = __abolition__
4. obstruct + ion = __obstruction__
5. construct + ion = __construction__
6. subtract + ion = __subtraction__
7. reflect + ion = __reflection__
8. retain + tion = __retention__
9. deflect + ion = __deflection__
10. revolve + tion = __revolution__
11. intersect + ion = __intersection__
12. attend + tion = __attention__
13. re + tribute + ion = __retribution__
14. institute + ion = __institution__

15. contradict + ion =
contradiction

17. retract + ion =
retraction

19. select + ion =
selection

16. instruct + ion =
instruction

18. contribute + ion =
contribution

20. detect + ion =
detection

Apply On the line, write the spelling word that is related by a common root or base word to each of the following words.

21. pollute — pollution

22. retracted — retraction

23. suggested — suggestions

24. contradicted — contradiction

25. attentive — attention

26. subtracted — subtraction

27. instructed — instruction

28. detectable — detection

29. intersected — intersection

30. contributed — contribution

Fill in the missing letters and write the resulting spelling words correctly on the lines below.

31. construc __tio__ n — construction

32. revo __lutio__ n — revolution

33. obstruc __tio__ n — obstruction

34. sele __ctio__ n — selection

35. refle __ctio__ n — reflection

36. rete __ntio__ n — retention

37. defl __ectio__ n — deflection

38. abol __itio__ n — abolition

39. instit __utio__ n — institution

40. retri __butio__ n — retribution

Spelling • *Skills Practice 2*

Name _____ **Date** _____

Formatting

Focus **Formatting** is how text is organized and presented on a printed page. The format can change depending on what you write and who your audience is. For example, a letter of request would not be formatted in the same way as a research report would be.

Practice **Choose the formatting term for a business letter that best fits in the sentences.**

heading	inside address	salutation
body	closing	signature

1. The _____closing_____ goes two lines below the body at the left margin.

2. Your _____signature_____ goes under the closing.

3. The _____heading_____ consists of the sender's address and the date. It goes in the upper left corner.

4. The _____salutation_____ is the greeting. A colon always goes after it.

5. The __inside address__ includes the name and address of the person receiving the letter. It goes two lines below the heading.

6. The _____body_____ is the main part of the letter. It contains what you want to say. It begins two lines below the salutation, and is single-spaced.

Apply Circle the letter of the answer that correctly completes each sentence about formatting an academic paper. You might want to have a word-processing program open during this exercise.

7. To add a header to your paper, you must first
   a. click View. **b.** open a new file. **c.** save your work.

8. The title of your paper should always be
   a. underlined. **b.** boldfaced. **c.** centered.

9. The empty spaces on the top, bottom, and sides of a paper are called
   a. tabs. **b.** headers. **c.** margins.

10. The font size tells you how big the
    a. spaces between lines will be. **b.** letters will be. **c.** page will be.

11. An academic paper should be
    a. single-spaced. **b.** double-spaced. **c.** triple-spaced.

12. To properly indent each paragraph, use
    a. the backspace key. **b.** the spacebar. **c.** the tab key.

13. To change the line spacing on text you have already written, you must first
    a. click Tools. **b.** close the file. **c.** highlight the text.

Name _____ Date _____

Word Origins, Prefix *inter-*, and Suffix *-sion*

Focus

Recognizing and understanding word origins can help you understand new and unfamiliar words. For example, the word *microscopic* appears in "The Mystery of Mars." It contains the Greek root *scop*. This root means "to look at." The prefix *micro-* means "very small." Thus *microscopic* literally means "too small to be seen."

The suffix *-sion* is used to change words into nouns.

comprehend + *-sion* = comprehension

propose + *-sion* = proposition

The prefix *inter-* means "between, among" or "through, across" when added to a base word.

inter- + planetary = interplanetary (across the distance between the planets)

inter- + session = intersession (between academic periods)

Practice

Write the definition of the word made from combining the root words and affixes provided.

1. Prefix *inter-*
Latin root: *rupt* meaning to break

Interrupt means <u>to cause something or someone to stop or be disturbed</u>

2. Prefix *inter-*
Latin root: *lude* meaning to play

Interlude means <u>piece of music played during a break</u>

3. Suffix *-sion*
Latin root: *div* meaning to separate

Division means <u>the act of splitting into parts</u>

Apply Write the word with the suffix *–sion* or the prefix *inter-* that best fits the definition. Then use each word in a sentence. Identify the base word, look up each word in the dictionary, and provide the origin of each base or root word.

international interstate	decision discussion	intergalactic intercept	confusion confession

4. Open debate of a question or topic <u>discussion</u>

Possible Answer <u>The class had a discussion about the science fair.</u>

<u>discuss from Latin literally meaning "to disperse"</u>

5. Going through several states <u>interstate</u>

Possible Answer <u>Our family always travels on interstate highways.</u>

<u>state from Latin literally meaning "to stand"</u>

6. Between or through galaxies <u>intergalactic</u>

Possible Answer <u>Fernando believed in the possibility of future</u>
intergalactic travel.
<u>galaxy from Greek literally meaning "milk"</u>

7. Act or result of making up one's mind <u>decision</u>

Possible Answer <u>Josie always made the decision for the entire group.</u>

<u>decide, from Latin literally meaning "to cut off"</u>

8. Across or among several nations <u>international</u>

Possible Answer <u>John dreamed of being an international traveler when</u>
he grew up.
<u>nation from Latin literally meaning "birth" or "race"</u>

Name _____ **Date** _____

Selection Vocabulary

Focus

impact (im'•pakt') *n.* the force of one object striking against another (page 388)

deflated (di•flāt'•əd) *v.* past tense of **deflate:** to let the air out of something (page 388)

analyze (an'•ə•līz') *v.* to find out what something is made of by taking it apart (page 390)

texture (teks'•chər) *n.* the look and feel of something (page 390)

hospitable (hos•pi'•tə•bəl) *adj.* welcome and comfortable; friendly (page 390)

microscopic (mī•krə•skä'•pik) *adj.* so small it can be seen only through a microscope (page 390)

harsh (härsh') *adj.* severe (page 391)

haze (hāz) *n.* mist, smoke, or dust in the air (page 392)

accumulate (ə'•kyūm'•yə•lāt') *v.* to gather or pile up (page 393)

pressure (pre'•shər) *n.* force caused by one thing pushing against another thing (page 394)

Practice   **Write the word that best fits each clue below.**

1. I drove over a nail, and my tire went flat. What did the nail

do to the tire? _____ deflated it _____

2. My aunt invited me to her home and fed me a delicious home-cooked

meal. Which word describes my aunt? _____ hospitable _____

3. This word describes the rough feel of sandpaper. Which word is it? _____texture_____

4. The desert air was extremely hot and the heat was severe. Which word describes the desert weather? _____harsh_____

5. This word can describe germs, cells, and bacteria. Which word is it? _____microscopic_____

6. Morgan and Mariah pushed on the jammed door to try to open it. What were they using? _____pressure_____

7. The dirty clothes are starting to pile up in the laundry room. Which word describes this? _____accumulate_____

8. Scientists do this to accumulated data. What do they do? _____analyze_____

9. The morning fog casts this over everything. What does it cast? _____haze_____

10. The force of the asteroid colliding with Earth left a crater. Which word describes the force? _____impact_____

Apply **Write the word that best matches the underlined word or phrase in the sentences below.**

11. The weather this winter has been <u>very severe</u>. _____harsh_____

12. The <u>look and feel</u> of sandpaper is rough. _____texture_____

13. The algae were <u>too small for us to see</u>. _____microscopic_____

14. Blair <u>let the air out of</u> the balloon. _____deflated_____

15. The <u>force</u> of the wrecking ball caused the building to collapse. _____impact_____

16. The <u>mist, smoke, or dust in the air</u> made my eyes water. _____haze_____

Name _____ **Date** _____

Making Conjectures

Our question or problem:

Possible Answer Should people colonize space and the

moon?

_____

_____

_____

_____

_____

Conjecture (my first theory or explanation):

Possible Answer I think we should colonize space and the

moon because we are going to run out of space on Earth.

_____

_____

_____

_____

_____

As you collect information, your conjecture will change. Return to
this page to record your new theories or explanations about your
question or problem.

Establishing Investigation Needs

My group's question or problem:

Possible Answer Should we colonize space and the moon?

_____

_____

_____

Knowledge Needs—Information I need to find or figure out in
order to investigate the question or problem:

A. **Possible Answer** Is it possible to colonize space?

B. **Possible Answer** What are the benefits of colonizing space?

C. **Possible Answer** What are the drawbacks?

D. _____

E. _____

Source	Useful?	How?
Encyclopedias		
Books		
Magazines	yes	for information on the ethics of space
Newspapers		
Video and Audio Clips	yes	programs on energy conservation
Television		
Interviews, observations	yes	for other expert views
Museums	yes	information on colonizing space
Other:		

Name _____ Date _____

Science Fiction Story

Think

Audience: Who will read your science fiction story?

<u>Possible Answer</u> my friends _____

Purpose: What do you want your readers to think about your story?

<u>Possible Answer</u> I want my readers to find the story imaginative and suspenseful.

Prewriting **Use this graphic organizer to plan your story.**

Possible Answers

Title
Saving Aquario

Who
Jerri—astronaut, crew; Pisces—leader of Aquario
Where
aboard the spacecraft *The Fish* and on the planet Aquario
When
year 2058

Key Events
visit Aquario and see the suffering; amazed at the underwater cities the Aquarians have built; contact leaders on Earth and other planets

Conflict
The water-covered planet Aquario is losing its water. Aquarians cannot survive without water.

Resolution
The astronauts transport the Aquarians to Earth and other water-rich planets.

Revising
Use this checklist to revise your graphic organizer and plans.

- ☐ Is your story set in the future?
- ☐ Does your story include some kind of science or technology?
- ☐ Have you chosen a point of view?
- ☐ Does your story have a conflict or problem?
- ☐ Have you decided how the characters will resolve the conflict?
- ☐ Does your story have rising action and a climax?
- ☐ Does your story have a beginning, middle, and end?

Editing/Proofreading
Use this checklist to edit your graphic organizer.

- ☐ Are proper nouns capitalized?
- ☐ Have you spelled invented words and names consistently?
- ☐ If you have invented names for people or places, are the names believable?
- ☐ Do the key events of your story happen in a logical order?

Publishing
Use this checklist to write your first draft.

- ☐ Use the graphic organizer as a guide to write the first draft of your story.
- ☐ Share your first draft with others to get suggestions and feedback.

Name _____ **Date** _____

Spelling

Focus

- A prefix changes the meaning of the base word it precedes. Identifying prefixes and understanding their meanings can help you figure out the meaning and spelling of a difficult or unfamiliar word. The prefix **inter-** means "among" or "between." For example, *interstate* means "between states."

- The suffix **-ly** changes an adjective to an adverb— *sad* to *sadly,* for example. The spelling of the base word does not change, unless it ends in *y.* In this case, change the *y* to *i* and add the *-ly.*

- The suffix **-sion** is like the suffixes *-tion/-ion*. It means "the state or quality of," and is added to verbs to make them nouns, as in *decision.* The suffix *-sion* is often added to verbs that end in a long vowel plus *de—decide, decision.* Drop the *-de* and add the *-sion* ending.

Word List

1. international
2. erosion
3. quietly
4. interlock
5. perpetually
6. interweave
7. provision
8. formerly
9. directly
10. regularly
11. explosion
12. relatively
13. persuasion
14. intercoastal
15. corrosion
16. decision
17. interview
18. interstate
19. awkwardly
20. exclusion

Practice Add the prefix *inter-* to the following base words to form spelling words from the list. Write the words on the line.

1. inter + state = _interstate_

2. inter + view = _interview_

3. inter + weave = _interweave_

4. inter + national = _international_

5. inter + lock = _interlock_

6. inter + coastal = _intercoastal_

Add the suffixes -ly or -sion to the following base words to form spelling words from the list, and write them on the lines.

7. erode – de + sion =
erosion

8. regular + ly =
regularly

9. decide – de + sion =
decision

10. persuade – de + sion =
persuasion

11. quiet + ly =
quietly

12. provide – de + sion =
provision

13. direct + ly =
directly

14. relative + ly =
relatively

15. corrode – de + sion =
corrosion

16. former + ly =
formerly

17. exclude – de + sion =
exclusion

18. explode – de + sion =
explosion

19. awkward + ly =
awkwardly

20. perpetual + ly =
perpetually

 **Apply** On the line, write the spelling word that is related by a common root or base word to each of the following words.

21. eroded   _erosion_

22. locking   _interlock_

23. weaving   _interweave_

24. irregular   _regularly_

25. perpetual   _perpetually_

26. persuasive   _persuasion_

27. undecided   _decision_

28. coastline   _intercoastal_

29. former   _formerly_

30. explosive   _explosion_

31. relation   _relatively_

32. state   _interstate_

33. indirect   _directly_

34. nation   _international_

35. provide   _provision_

36. preview   _interview_

37. corroded   _corrosion_

38. excluded   _exclusion_

39. awkwardness   _awkwardly_

40. quietness   _quietly_

Name _____ Date _____

Independent and Dependent Clauses

Focus A **clause** is a group of words that has a subject and a verb.

Rule	**Example**
• An **independent clause** can stand alone as a sentence.	• I found the book in the fiction section.
• A **dependent clause** has a subject and a verb, but it cannot stand alone as a sentence.	• I found the book **that Julie needed for school** in the fiction section.
• **Dependent clauses** modify words in sentences. They are used as either adjectives or adverbs.	• *That Julie needed for school* modifies the noun *book*, so it is being used as an adjective.

Practice Label each example below with *I* for an independent clause or *D* for a dependent clause.

1. __I__ That dog always makes me nervous.

2. __D__ Because Mr. Gupta usually rides the subway.

3. __D__ After the rain began pouring down.

4. __I__ Aaron likes to go biking.

5. __D__ That Paul wanted to purchase.

Apply The following sentences contain independent and dependent clauses. Circle each dependent clause and underline each independent clause. Remember to look for relative pronouns and subordinating conjunctions as clues.

6. Thanh will go to the state finals (if he wins the next match.)

7. The volcano, (which people thought was dormant,) began rumbling loudly.

8. (Unless you study,) you might not pass the test.

9. After school, Marika walks to the bakery (where her mother works.)

10. The astronauts traveled (where no other humans had gone before.)

11. (Because there were so many mosquitoes,) we moved our picnic inside.

12. The man (whose truck blocked our driveway) apologized to my mom.

13. Clio was not allowed to go to the movies (until she cleaned her room.)

14. The place (that Devon visited most often) was the library.

15. The planet Mars is (where I would like to live someday.)

Name _____ **Date** _____

Synonyms and Antonyms

Antonyms are words with opposite, or nearly opposite, meanings. An antonym for *empty* is *full,* and an antonym for *dull* is *exciting.*

Synonyms are words with the same, or nearly the same, meaning. A synonym for *empty* is *vacant,* and a synonym for *dull* is *boring.*

Practice Each word below is followed by two words. Circle the *antonym.*

1. extraordinary   rare   (normal)

2. anchored   (moving)   fixed

3. left   (joined)   departed

4. captured   trapped   (released)

5. drop   fall   (climb)

6. loud   (silent)   noisy

Each word below is followed by two words. Circle the synonym.

7. lost   (misplaced)   found

8. built   destroyed   (constructed)

9. remote   nearby   (distant)

10. tense   (stressed)   relaxed

11. carefully   (cautiously)   recklessly

12. completely   partly   (entirely)

Apply   **Write a new sentence using an antonym for the underlined word in each sentence below. Underline the antonym you used in your sentence.**

13. Nitesh's <u>usual</u> lunch consisted of a sandwich and a piece of fruit.

   Possible Answer As a <u>special</u> treat, my family went to an arcade, and we ate pizza.

14. The attorney visited the office to discuss a <u>serious</u> legal issue.

   Possible Answer Comedians always have <u>funny</u> stories to tell.

Write a new sentence using a synonym for the underlined word in each sentence below. Underline the synonym you used in your sentence.

15. It is important to stay <u>focused</u> when you are taking a test.

   Possible Answer The dog was <u>alert</u> to a squirrel running along the top of the fence.

16. The car's <u>exterior</u> was dented and scratched, but the engine worked fine.

   Possible Answer The <u>outside</u> of my house is painted pink—my favorite color.

Name _____ **Date** _____

Selection Vocabulary

Focus

module (mä'•jəl) *n.* a part of a spacecraft that has a special use and can be separated from the rest of the craft (page 406)

bulky (bəl'•kē) *adj.* large and puffy (page 406)

focused (fō•kəst) *v.* past tense of **focus:** to direct attention to someone or something (page 408)

thrust (thrust) *n.* a sudden, strong push or force (page 410)

hatch (hach) *n.* an opening in the deck of a ship or spacecraft that leads to other decks (page 413)

tranquility (tran•kwil'•ə•tē) *n.* the absence of motion or disturbance (page 414)

awe (ô) *n.* great wonder, fear, and respect (page 421)

depressed (di•prest') *v.* past tense of **depress:** to be sunk below the surrounding region (page 420)

mankind (man'•kīnd) *n.* human beings as a group; the human race (page 422)

sensations (sen•sā'•shənz) *n.* plural of **sensation:** feeling (page 422)

Practice Write the word from the word box that matches each definition below.

sensations	module	awe	depressed
thrust	bulky	focused	tranquility
	mankind	hatch	

1. _____awe_____ great wonder, fear, and respect

2. _____depressed_____ sunk below the surrounding area

3. _____bulky_____ large and puffy

4. _____mankind_____ human beings as a group

5. _____thrust_____ a sudden, strong push or force

6. _____tranquility_____ the absence of motion or disturbance

7. _____focused_____ directed attention to someone or something

8. _____module_____ a part of a spacecraft that has a special use and can be separated from the rest of the craft

9. _____sensations_____ feelings

10. _____hatch_____ an opening in the deck of a ship or spacecraft that leads to other decks

Apply Write the vocabulary word that best matches the underlined word or phrase in the sentences below.

11. When Julia caught a glimpse of the Grand Canyon, she was filled with wonder and amazement _____awe_____

12. I had many happy feelings when my younger sister was born. _____sensations_____

13. Audrey climbed through the opening in the deck of a spacecraft and prepared for her spacewalk. _____hatch_____

14. We could feel the sudden, strong force when the roller coaster took off. _____thrust_____

Name _____ Date _____

Drawing Conclusions

Focus Writers cannot describe every detail about people or events in a story. Good readers draw conclusions using the information they have been given. **Drawing conclusions** means using the information in the text to make a statement about a person or event. The conclusion is not stated by the author, but the information in the text supports it.

Practice Reread pages 416–417 of *"Apollo 11: First Moon Landing."* What conclusion can you draw about Neil Armstrong based on the text? Write your conclusion below, and then support it with information from the text.

Conclusion:

Possible Answer Armstrong knew how to react in a crisis.

Information that supports my conclusion:

1. **Possible Answer** When Armstrong saw boulders at the landing site, he quickly took control of the module away from the computer.

2. **Possible Answer** Armstrong did not ask Houston what he should do, he just did it.

Apply Think of someone you admire, and then write a paragraph below showing why you look up to this person. Do not say how you feel. Instead, provide information that leads a reader to conclude that your subject is someone you admire.

Possible Answer Mr. Kwan owns a bakery at the end of my block. Each night, after the store has closed, he places the unsold loaves of bread into a box. I have helped him do this a couple of times. Then he drives to the local food pantry and donates the bread.

Name _____ **Date** _____

Science Fiction Story

Think

Audience: Who will read your science fiction story?

<u>**Possible Answer** my friends</u>

Purpose: What do you want your readers to think about your story?

<u>**Possible Answer** I want my readers to find the story</u>
imaginative and suspenseful.

Revising

Once you have written the first draft of your story, share it with others to get their feedback. You can decide whether or not to use their ideas, but listen carefully to each one. Someone may have the perfect solution to a problem you are having with your story. On the lines below, write three ideas you were given to improve your story. Then decide how you will use each one.

Possible Answer

1. Suggestion: <u>There should be another main character from the</u>
<u>planet Aquario.</u>

Decision: <u>I will add an Aquarian named Neptune.</u>

2. Suggestion: <u>Aquario should blow up at the end of the story.</u>

_____

Decision: <u>I do not want to use this suggestion.</u>

3. Suggestion: <u>It is unclear why Aquario is losing its water.</u>

_____

Decision: <u>I will explain that Aquario is orbiting too close to its sun.</u>

Revising

Use this checklist to revise your story.

☐ Is the point of view consistent throughout your story?

☐ Does your opening sentence grab the reader's attention?

☐ Have you created vivid characters with your descriptions?

☐ Do the events of your plot occur in a logical sequence?

☐ Does the tension rise as your story moves toward the climax? Have you added foreshadowing?

Editing/Proofreading

Use this checklist to correct mistakes.

☐ Did you use a thesaurus to find precise and descriptive words?

☐ Did the spelling of invented words remain the same throughout your story?

☐ Have you corrected run-on sentences and fragments?

☐ Did you correctly place quotation marks in your dialogue?

☐ Did you correctly use commas to separate clauses in complex sentences?

Publishing

Use this checklist to prepare your story for publication.

☐ Rewrite your story neatly in your best cursive handwriting.

☐ Illustrate your story with drawings, clip art, or other graphics.

Name _____ **Date** _____

Spelling

Focus
- **Synonyms** are words with the same, or nearly the same, meaning. For example, *cold* and *chilly* are synonyms.

- **Antonyms** are words with opposite, or nearly opposite, meanings. For example, *cheap* and *expensive* are antonyms.

You can find synonyms and antonyms for words in a thesaurus. Use synonyms and antonyms to help you remember the meaning of a new word.

Word List
1. graceful
2. prohibit
3. exceed
4. opposition
5. fatigue
6. distant
7. forbid
8. restrict
9. secluded
10. surpass
11. commencement
12. similarity
13. energy
14. outlandish
15. difference
16. conclusion
17. alliance
18. strange
19. clumsy
20. remote

Practice On the lines, write the groups of words from the word list that are synonyms. Use a thesaurus or dictionary if necessary. **Possible Answers**

1. exceed
2. surpass
3. strange
4. outlandish
5. remote
6. distant
7. secluded
8. prohibit
9. forbid
10. restrict

On the lines, write the pairs of words from the word list that are antonyms. Use a thesaurus or dictionary if necessary. Possible Answers

11. clumsy   15. energy   19. commencement

12. graceful   16. fatigue   20. conclusion

13. similarity   17. opposition

14. difference   18. alliance

Apply For each word below, list the spelling words that are synonyms on the lines. Use a thesaurus or dictionary if necessary.
Possible Answers

isolated   **ban**

1. remote   6. prohibit

2. distant   7. forbid

3. secluded   8. restrict

weird   **outdo**

4. strange   9. exceed

5. outlandish   10. surpass

For each word below, write the spelling word that is a synonym in the synonym column. Then write the spelling word that is an antonym in the antonym column. Use a thesaurus or dictionary if necessary.

Possible Answers	Synonym	Antonym
11. beginning	commencement	conclusion
12. liveliness	energy	fatigue
13. likeness	similarity	difference
14. partnership	alliance	opposition
15. awkward	clumsy	graceful

Name _____ Date _____

Apostrophes and Quotation Marks

Focus **Apostrophes** are used to show possession and to form contractions.

- For most singular nouns, add 's.
- cat's ears, boss's necktie

- For plural nouns that end with s, add an apostrophe.
- flowers' petals
  troops' uniforms

- For singular proper nouns that end in s, add 's.
- the Harris's backyard
  Chris's haircut

A **contraction** is formed by combining two words and omitting one or more letters. An apostrophe replaces the missing letters.

do not, don't   we will, we'll   you have, you've

- **Quotation marks** are used to enclose a direct quotation. Periods and commas go inside the quotation marks.

- Place the exclamation point or question mark inside the quotation marks when it is part of the quotation, and outside when it is part of the entire sentence.

Example: The librarian asked, "Please be quiet."

Practice **Add quotation marks and apostrophes to the following sentences where needed.**

1. "What kind of vegetables don't you like?" asked Mom.

2. Didn't Mom say, "Watch your brother"?

3. The announcer said, "The game's officially over."

4. Gary shouted, "Stay with Louis' dog!"

5. "Hard work's the key to success," Dad's boss always says.

Apply The apostrophes and quotation marks in the following sentences are missing or used incorrectly. Rewrite each sentence correctly.

6. King George did'nt need anyones help reading John Hancocks' giant signature.

"King George didn't need anyone's help reading John Hancock's giant signature!."

7. Our teacher said, Because of Americas constitution, "wer'e guaranteed certain rights that ca'nt be taken away."

Our teacher said, "Because of America's constitution, we're guaranteed certain rights that can't be taken away."

8. Would youve been for the "Rebel's or the Tories'" during the Revolution? Rufus asked.

"Would you've been for the Rebels or the Tories during the Revolution?" Rufus asked.

9. Riding hi"s horse as fast as he could, Paul Revere shouted, 'The British are coming!'

Riding his horse as fast as he could, Paul Revere shouted, "The British are coming!"

10. Thomas Paines writings weren"t very popular in "England", said Mr. Stevens.

"Thomas Paine's writings weren't very popular in England," said Mr. Stevens.

Name _____ **Date** _____

Homographs and the Prefix *photo-*

Focus **Homographs** are words that are spelled the same but have different meanings and different origins. Sometimes homographs have different pronunciations because the stress is placed on a different syllable.

The prefix *photo-* is from Greek meaning "light." Read the literal meaning of the following word with the prefix *photo-:*

Photo- + meter = to measure light

Practice **Write the word with the prefix *photo-* that matches each definition below.**

photocopy	photosynthesis	photometer

1. Copy of printed material made through the action of light

_____ photocopy _____

2. Synthesizing food for plants with the aid of light __photosynthesis__

3. Instrument used for measuring the intensity of light ____photometer____

Identify the base word used above that is a homograph and write two of the word's meanings.

meter_____

Possible Answer unit of length; poetic rhythm

_____

Apply Circle the homographs in the sentences below. Remember that some homographs have different pronunciations. Write the definition of the word as used in the sentence on the line. Using the word with the prefix *photo-* listed, write another sentence using one of the homograph's alternate meanings.

4. The president will (address) the people on television.

photograph **Possible Answer** I took a photograph of my family after we had moved to our current address.

5. We were (content) to lie on the beach all day.

photosynthesis **Possible Answer** The contents of plants make photosynthesis possible.

6. The (desert) is a dry place with miles of sand.

photoelectric **Possible Answer** The old photoelectric lab had been deserted years earlier.

7. He would set the tape player to (record) his favorite radio program.

photocopy **Possible Answer** It is always a good idea to photocopy your important records in case you lose them.

8. The woman used a (file) to smooth the customer's fingernails.

photogenic **Possible Answer** At the agency, the files were filled with pictures of photogenic people.

Name _____   Date _____

Selection Vocabulary

Focus

transferring (trans•fûr'•ing) *v.* moving from one place to another (page 434)

responsibilities (ri•spon'•sə•bil'•i•tēz) *n.* plural of **responsibility:** something that is a person's job, duty, or concern (page 434)

confidence (kon'•fi•dəns) *n.* faith in oneself (page 434)

discouraged (di•skûr'•ijd) *v.* past tense of **discourage:** to try to keep a person from doing something (page 437)

application (ap'•li•kā'•shən) *n.* a request, especially for a job (page 437)

processes (prä'•se•səz') *n.* plural of **process:** a series of actions performed in making or doing something (page 438)

eclipse (i•klips') *n.* a darkening or hiding of the sun, a planet, or a moon, by another heavenly body (page 441)

precise (pri•sīs') *adj.* exact; definite (page 442)

varies (vâr'•ēz) *v.* changes; makes or becomes different (page 442)

advance (ad•vans') *v.* to help the progress or growth of; further (page 444)

Practice   Complete each sentence below with a word from the box.

precise	confidence	processes	varies	advance
transferring	discouraged	application	eclipse	responsibilities

1. Maxwell was _____discouraged_____ from going outside by the heat.

2. Today I mailed my _____application_____ for enrolling in a local music school.

3. The measurements need to be _____precise_____ so that the frame will fit the picture.

4. The amount of produce needed _____varies_____ depending on the recipe.

5. Niki reached out to _____advance_____ her pawn and knocked over her queen.

6. My _____responsibilities_____ include sweeping the kitchen and taking out the trash.

7. Whenever he sits at the piano, Cameron is filled with _____confidence_____.

8. As I am _____transferring_____ this dirt to the pot, will you hold the plant?

9. Orlando looked through a special lens to view the _____eclipse_____.

10. There are a number of _____processes_____ involved in turning oil into gasoline.

Apply Write a vocabulary word next to the group of words that have a similar meaning.

11. changes; alters; diverse _____varies_____

12. procedures; steps; moves _____processes_____

13. sureness; courage; self-reliance _____confidence_____

14. further; promote; support _____advance_____

15. clear; accurate; explicit _____precise_____

16. sending; carrying; conveying _____transferring_____

17. hindered; prevented; deterred _____discouraged_____

18. duties; obligations; burdens _____responsibilities_____

Name _____ **Date** _____

Research Report: Biography

 Audience: **Who** will read your biography?

<u>**Possible Answer** someone interested in my subject</u>

Purpose: **What** is your reason for writing a biography?
<u>**Possible Answer** I want to share information about an influential</u>
<u>person.</u>

Prewriting **Use this time line to plan your biography. Remember that a biography can cover a person's entire life, or just an important period in that person's life. Use a separate piece of paper to add more boxes if necessary.** Possible Answers

Subject of Time Line: <u>Guion Bluford</u>

Date	Event
<u>1966</u>	<u>Bluford flew for the U.S. Air Force during the Vietnam War.</u>
<u>1978</u>	<u>Bluford earned his Ph.D. in aerospace engineering.</u>
<u>1979</u>	<u>Bluford became a NASA astronaut.</u>
<u>1983</u>	<u>Bluford became the first African American in space when</u> <u>he flew on the space shuttle *Challenger* for mission STS-8.</u>
<u>1997</u>	<u>Bluford was inducted into the Space Hall of Fame.</u>

Revising — Use this checklist to revise your research.

☐ Have you checked resources like magazines, Web sites, interviews, and videos or DVDs?

☐ Do you have enough information to create an informative research report?

☐ Are the events in your time line listed in chronological order?

☐ Are there cause-and-effect relationships between events in your subject's life?

☐ Have you decided whether you will write about your subject's entire life or focus on a single event?

☐ Did you rewrite the information you found in your own words?

Editing/Proofreading — Use this checklist to correct mistakes.

☐ Did you include bibliographic information for each source?

☐ Did you use quotation marks if you needed to quote someone's exact words?

☐ Did you check the spellings of proper names or specialized words against the original source?

☐ Did you check proper nouns and quotations to make sure they are capitalized correctly?

Publishing — Use this checklist to see if you are ready to begin writing your report.

☐ Is the information you have found organized so that your report will have a beginning, middle, and end?

☐ Have you chosen a point of view for your report?

Name _____ **Date** _____

Spelling

Focus
- **Root words** were formed from words of other languages, such as Greek and Latin. Understanding and identifying root words and their meanings can help you spell many new words. Here are some roots in the spelling words and their meanings:

loc = "place"; *fac* = "make" or "do"; *graph* = "write"; *pop* = "people"; *vac* = "empty"; *photo* = "light"; *man* = "hand"; *bene* = "well," or "good"; *aut* or *auto* = "self," or "same"; *geo* = "earth"

Practice Fill in the root word and write the resulting spelling word on the line. Use each spelling word only once.

1. dis + ___loc___ + ate =   dislocate
2. manu + ___fac___ + ture =   manufacture
3. ___graph___ + ic =   graphic
4. ___pop___ + ular =   popular
5. e + ___vac___ + uate =   evacuate
6. ___vac___ + ate =   vacate
7. auto + ___graph___ =   autograph
8. ___fac___ + tory =   factory
9. ___geo___ + graphy =   geography
10. ___pop___ + ulation =   population
11. vac or loc + ation =   vacation or location
12. loc or vac + ation =   vacation or location
13. ___pop___ + ulated =   populated

Word List
1. geography
2. dislocate
3. manufacture
4. locality
5. evacuate
6. allocate
7. benefactor
8. graphic
9. populated
10. photograph
11. location
12. vacate
13. popular
14. vacant
15. population
16. graphite
17. vacancy
18. factory
19. vacation
20. autograph

14. ___vac___ + ancy =   vacancy

15. al + ___loc___ + ate =   allocate

16. ___loc___ + ality =   locality

17. ___pop___ + ular =   popular

18. bene + ___fac___ + tor =   benefactor

19. ___graph___ + ite =   graphite

20. ___vac___ + ant =   vacant

Apply Write the spelling word that is represented by the following root word meaning combinations.

Example: at a distance + to see = *television*

21. hand + to make + *ture* =   manufacture

22. self + to write =   autograph

23. light + to write =   photograph

24. well or good + to make + *tor* =   benefactor

25. earth + to write + *y* =   geography

Choose the word that does *not* share the same main root word as the other two and write it on the line.

26. evacuate, populated, vacant   populated

27. locality, allocate, factory   factory

28. graphite, geography, evacuate   evacuate

29. photograph, allocate, graphite   allocate

30. popular, vacancy, population   vacancy

31. graphic, graphite, vacate   vacate

32. location, locality, vacation   vacation

33. manufacture, benefactor, location   location

34. vacant, graphite, autograph   vacant

35. populated, dislocate, popular   dislocate

Name _____ Date _____

Subject and Verb Agreement, Run-on Sentences, and Fragments

Focus The verb used in a sentence must agree with the subject.

- Add *-s* or *-es* to present tense verbs when they are singular.

- Do not add *s* or *es* to present tense verbs when they are plural or used with *I* or *you.*

- He **waits** at the table for his lunch.

- They **wait** at the table.
  I **wait** at the table.
  You **wait** at the table.

- **Run-on sentences** are two or more complete sentences written as though they are one.

- **Fragments** are groups of words that do not express a complete thought. A fragment is missing a subject, a predicate, or both.

Practice Read each pair of sentences below. Place a check mark next to the sentence that has subject and verb agreement. Also, identify each as Run-on (R), Fragment (F), or Complete (C).

1. __R__ I stays with my aunt on Saturday my Grandfather on Sunday.

   __✓__ I stay with my aunt on Saturday my Grandfather on Sunday.

2. __✓ C__ Lisbeth and her sister throw a big party each year on the Fourth of July.

   _____ Lisbeth and her sister throws a big party each year on the Fourth of July.

3. __✓ F__ It smells funny.

   _____ It smell funny.

4. __R__ Wendy and Ramona leaves on Monday Ronnie is never leaving.

   __✓__ Wendy and Ramona leave on Monday Ronnie is never leaving.

Apply Rewrite each sentence, correcting subject-verb agreement and, if necessary, making it a complete sentence.

Possible Answers

5. Paul go to the store his friends stays home.

Paul goes to the store, and his friends stay home.

6. Because our family like pie.

We don't eat cake because our family likes pie.

7. After Julius wents to the tennis match.

After Julius went to the tennis match, he went home.

8. The gas station down the street are closed today.

The gas station down the street is closed today.

9. The child play in the backyard the parents prepares for the celebration.

The child plays in the backyard while the parents prepare for the celebration.

10. Tony sing beautifully.

Tony sings beautifully.

11. Shirley and Loretta always agrees Ward and James never does.

Shirley and Loretta always agree, but Ward and James never do.

12. He walk as fast as I can.

He walks as fast as I can.

13. Our turtles loves taking baths our gerbil take sand baths.

Our turtles love taking baths, and our gerbil takes sand baths.

14. My sister who live in Chicago move to a different apartment every year.

My sister who lives in Chicago moves to a different apartment every year.

15. All the fishermen sail away they'll come back with nets full of fish.

All the fishermen sailed away, and they'll come back with nets full of fish.

Name _____ **Date** _____

Words with Latin Roots

Latin roots are common in the English language. Identifying and understanding Latin roots can help you define difficult and unfamiliar words. When you know the meaning of a root, you can figure out the meanings of many words that contain that root.

Practice The following words with Latin roots were taken from "Buffalo Hunt." Each word is followed by the root word and its definition. Think of other words that use each Latin root and write them on the line.

Possible Answers

1. supported

port: carry ___transport, import, portable___

2. described

scrib: write ___subscribe, inscribe, scribble___

3. dependent

pend: hang ___pendant, pendulum, appendix___

4. signal

sign: mark ___designate, design, signature___

5. sufficient

fic: make ___fiction, efficient, artificial___

Apply The following groups of words all have the same Latin roots. Circle the root that each word has in common. Then examine each word carefully and think of its definition. You may need to look up some words in a dictionary or thesaurus. Think about what the definitions have in common. Then write what you think each root means.

6. structure, reconstruction, destruction, instruct

   The Latin root is **struct.** What does **struct** mean? __to build__

7. tribute, contribute, tributary, attribute

   The Latin root is **trib.** What does **trib** mean? __to give__

8. reflex, flexible, flexor

   The Latin root is **flex.** What does **flex** mean? __to bend__

9. dentist, dental, dentistry

   The Latin root is **dent.** What does **dent** mean? __tooth__

10. narrate, narrator, narrative

    The Latin root is **narr.** What does **narr** mean? __tell__

Word Structure • *Skills Practice 2*

Name _____   **Date** _____

Selection Vocabulary

Focus

legends (lej' · əndz) *n.* plural of **legend:** a story passed down through the years that many people believe but that is not entirely true (page 465)

sacred (sā' · krid) *adj.* regarded as deserving respect (page 465)

stampede (stam · pēd') *v.* to cause a sudden, wild running of a frightened herd of animals (page 467)

banners (ban' · ûrz) *n.* plural of **banner:** a piece of cloth that has a design and sometimes writing on it (page 471)

lurking (lûr' · king) *adj.* lying hidden and quiet, preparing to attack (page 472)

procession (prə · sesh' · ən) *n.* a group of people moving forward in a line or in a certain order (page 472)

elders (el' · dərz) *n.* plural of **elder:** a person who is older (page 474)

cow (kou) *n.* the fully grown female of some large mammals such as buffaloes, elephants, and whales (page 478)

ladles (lā' · dəlz) *n.* plural of **ladle:** a spoon with a long handle and a bowl shaped like a cup. It is used to scoop up liquids (page 481)

pitched (pitchd) *v.* past tense of **pitch:** to set up (page 482)

Practice   **Circle the word in parentheses that best fits each sentence.**

1. Our (legends/elders) gave us advice about the future.

2. Melissa created colorful (reservations/banners) for the game.

3. The loud thunder started a (stampede/lurking) of the wild horses.

4. Gabriela read about the (procession/legends) of the ancient people.

5. Jesse quickly (pitched/deserted) the tent before it rained.

6. There were (banners/ladles) by every pot of soup.

7. These old books are (sacred/lurking) to our family.

8. (Lurking/Elders) in the trees, the snake waited for its prey to come.

9. The female elephant lost track of her pack, but the (cow/banners) soon found them.

10. The (procession/stampede) traveled through the city square as the entire town watched.

Apply   **Write *T* in the blank if the sentence for the vocabulary word is correct. Write *F* if the sentence is false. For every *F* answer, write the vocabulary word that fits the definition.**

11. *Elders* are stories passed down through the years that

many people believe but that are not entirely true. ___F___

___Legends___

12. *Ladles* are pieces of cloth with a design and sometimes writing

on them. ___F___ ___Banners___

13. *Pitched* means "to set up." ___T___ _____

14. A *procession* is a sudden, wild running of a frightened herd

of animals. ___F___ ___stampede___

15. When someone is *lurking,* he or she is lying hidden and quiet,

as if preparing to attack. ___T___ _____

Name _____ Date _____

Recording Concept Information

As I read each selection, this is what I added to my understanding of the unit theme Going West. **Possible Answers**

- "Buffalo Hunt" by Russell Freedman I learned that Native American Indians had thriving civilizations before people migrated West. They had an interconnected relationship with the land and the death of the buffalo contributed to their society collapsing.

- "The Journal of Wong Ming-Chung" by Lawrence Yep

I learned that the gold rush was a free for all for anyone to strike it rich. Many people including the Chinese were able to succeed and establish themselves.

- "Bill Pickett: Rodeo-Ridin' Cowboy" by Andrea Pinkney

I learned that black cowboys were separated from white cowboys and that Bill Pickett's success seemed to help people realize that black cowboys can be equally talented horsemen.

- "Ghost Towns of the American West" by Raymond Bial

I learned that not everyone succeeded who went West. The towns were put up quickly and died quickly as the natural resources were exploited.

- "McBroom the Rainmaker" by Sid Fleischman

I learned that tall tales were a form of entertainment before television. The people who traveled West saw some pretty fantastic landscapes, animals, and weather, and the tales seem to be an exaggeration of these things.

Knowledge about Going West

• This is what I know about going west before reading the unit.

Possible Answer People moved west to settle the land. They
cleared the land and set up farms and towns. They fought
with the Native Americans because they were competing for
the same resources.

• These are some things about going west that I would like to
talk about and understand better.

Possible Answer Why were Native Americans moved to
reservations? What was life like in the old west?

Reminder: I should read this page again when I get to the
end of the unit to see how much my ideas about going west
have changed.

Name _____ Date _____

Ideas about Going West

Of the ideas discussed in class about going west, these are the ones I found most interesting.

Possible Answer Many different kinds of people took part in the history of the American West. Chinese immigrants, African Americans, and Native Americans were just as much a part of the time and place as cowboys and prospectors.

_____

_____

_____

_____

_____

_____

_____

_____

_____

_____

_____

_____

_____

_____

Ideas about Going West (continued)

Write down the ideas you found most interesting about the selection "Buffalo Hunt." Discuss your ideas with the class.

Possible Answer The Buffalo were central to the lives of

Native Americans. We can see how with the loss of the

buffalo, the Native Americans lost much of their culture and

way of life.

_____

_____

_____

_____

_____

_____

_____

_____

_____

_____

_____

Name _____ Date _____

Describing Two Objects

**Think**

Audience: Who will read your description?

Possible Answer another student

Purpose: What do you want your description to do?

Possible Answer I want the reader to be able to clearly picture the objects I have described.

Prewriting **Visualize the objects you want to describe. This method will help you focus on the most important details. Your description should be vivid and detailed. Remember to use descriptions that appeal to the five senses. Use the following graphic organizer to help you start your descriptive writing.**

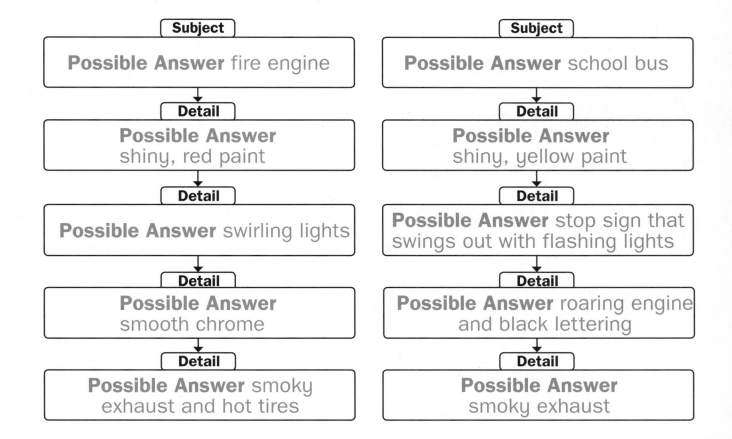

Subject	Subject
Possible Answer fire engine	**Possible Answer** school bus
Detail	**Detail**
Possible Answer shiny, red paint	**Possible Answer** shiny, yellow paint
Detail	**Detail**
Possible Answer swirling lights	**Possible Answer** stop sign that swings out with flashing lights
Detail	**Detail**
Possible Answer smooth chrome	**Possible Answer** roaring engine and black lettering
Detail	**Detail**
Possible Answer smoky exhaust and hot tires	**Possible Answer** smoky exhaust

Revising
Use this checklist to revise your description.

- ☐ Did you include enough concrete sensory details?
- ☐ Are your details grouped in a way that makes sense?
- ☐ Have you chosen vivid and descriptive words?
- ☐ Have you used similes or metaphors?
- ☐ Will your audience know what you are describing?

Editing/Proofreading
Use this checklist to edit your description.

- ☐ Do the verb tenses you used make sense?
- ☐ Have you correctly used appositives?
- ☐ Have you checked your description for spelling errors?
- ☐ Have you used correct punctuation and capitalization?

Publishing
Use this checklist to publish your description.

- ☐ Write neatly or type on a computer to create a final copy.
- ☐ Share your description with other students.

Name _____ **Date** _____

Spelling

Focus

- **Homophones** are words that sound the same but have different spellings and different meanings. The following word pairs are examples of homophones.
  clause, claws; wade, weighed; stationary, stationery

- Understanding and identifying **Latin roots** and their meanings can help you define and spell difficult and unfamiliar words. Here are some of the Latin roots in the spelling words and their meanings: ***terr*** = "land" or "earth"; ***ver*** = "truth"; ***tain*** and ***ten*** = "hold"

Word List

1. clause
2. claws
3. wade
4. weighed
5. stationary
6. stationery
7. overseas
8. oversees
9. lightening
10. lightning
11. terrain
12. terrace
13. territory
14. territorial
15. verdict
16. verify
17. verity
18. retain
19. contain
20. detain

Practice — On the line, write the homophone from the spelling list after its brief definition.

1. part of a sentence — clause
2. animal or bird nails — claws
3. flash of light in the sky — lightning
4. making less heavy — lightening
5. across the ocean — overseas
6. watches over — oversees
7. paper for writing letters — stationery
8. not moving — stationary
9. walk through shallow water — wade
10. measured the heaviness of — weighed

Using the Latin roots provided, write the spelling words that are formed when the Latin root is added. Use each spelling word only once.

terr

11. _____ace   terrace

12. _____itorial   territorial

13. _____itory   territory

tain

14. re_____   retain

15. de_____   detain

16. con_____   contain

Apply Circle the misspellings, or incorrect homophones, in the sentences below. Write the misspelled words correctly on the lines provided. If there are no misspelled words in a sentence, write *correct.*

17. A flash of (lightening) lit up the sky.

18. That cat has sharp (clause)

19. The letter was written on fine (stationary)

20. The soldier had been (oversees) for a year.

lightning
claws
stationery
overseas

If the spelling word in the sentence is misspelled, write the correct spelling of the word on the line. If it is correct, write *correct.*

21. The covered wagon traveled over rough turrain.

22. Please do not detane us any longer.

23. Has the jury decided on a verdict yet?

24. Will you varify your address?

25. There are all kinds of plants on the tarrace.

26. What does that bowl containe?

terrain
detain
correct
verify
terrace
contain

Name _____ **Date** _____

Verb Tense and Sentence Tense

**Focus**

- **Present tense** = action happening now or on a regular basis.

- **Past tense** = action that has already happened.

- **Future tense** = action that will happen. Use *will* or *shall* with the main verb.

- I **feel** a mosquito on my neck. Sean **feels** relief whenever he finishes a math test.

- Jamie **felt** bad when her favorite sports team lost.

- John **will feel** relaxed as soon as his vacation begins.

Practice Read each sentence below. Then circle the letter of the verb tense the sentence contains.

1. The waves rolled onto the beach and swept away the sand castle bit by bit.

   a. future tense   **b.** present tense   **c.** past tense

2. A school bus will take our class to a museum on Thursday.

   a. past tense   **b.** present tense   **c.** future tense

3. Maddy eats a peanut butter sandwich for lunch nearly every day.

   a. present tense   **b.** past tense   **c.** future tense

4. At the end of the year, Shonda will complete her second year of piano lessons.

   a. present tense   **b.** future tense   **c.** past tense

5. Yesterday, I went to the mall to buy my sister a birthday present.

   a. present tense   **b.** past tense   **c.** future tense

Apply Read the following sentences. If the verb tenses used in the sentence make sense, place a check mark on the line. If they do not make sense, rewrite the sentence using the correct tense for the underlined verb on the lines provided.

6. _____ Whenever Aunt Lucy traveled, she <u>makes</u> at least one new friend.

   Whenever Aunt Lucy traveled, she made at least one new friend.

7. ✓ If the city decides to widen the road, workers <u>will chop</u> down that tree.

   _____

   _____

8. _____ The students have planned a going-away party for Allison, who <u>moved</u> to Las Vegas tomorrow.

   The students have planned a going-away party for Allison, who will move to Las Vegas tomorrow.

9. _____ A truck rumbled down the street, and an airplane <u>has flown</u> overhead.

   A truck rumbled down the street, and an airplane flew overhead.

10. ✓ We will finish this lesson next week, so you <u>will need</u> to have the new book by then.

   _____

   _____

Name _____ **Date** _____

Suffix -*ent*

Focus The suffix -***ent*** means "having the quality of." When it is added to a root word, it usually forms an adjective.

**Practice** Change each boldfaced word below to form the word with the suffix -*ent* that matches the definition.

1. has the quality of **depending**

   dependent

2. has the quality of **differing**

   different

3. has the quality of **emerging**

   emergent

4. has the quality of **appearing** clearly

   apparent

5. has the quality of **absorbing**

   absorbent

Apply Choose the word from the word bank that matches the definitions.

competent convenient	insistent excellent	permanent complacent	intelligent efficient	negligent apparent

6. nearby or easily accessible ___convenient___

7. having the quality of excelling ___excellent___

8. having the quality of competence ___competent___

9. having the quality of permanence ___permanent___

10. having the quality of insisting ___insistent___

11. having the quality of being satisfied or pleased ___complacent___

12. having the quality of being visible or easily understood
    ___apparent___

13. having the quality of being productive without being wasteful
    ___efficient___

14. having the quality of being smart or having intelligence
    ___intelligent___

15. having the quality of being careless or showing neglect
    ___negligent___

Name _____ Date _____

Selection Vocabulary

Focus

immigrants (i'·mi·grənts) *n.* plural of **immigrant:** a person who comes to live in a country in which he or she was not born (page 498)

endure (in·dûr') *v.* to put up with (page 498)

rationed (rash'·ənd) *v.* past tense of **ration:** to limit to fixed portions (page 499)

burden (bûr'·dən) *n.* something hard to bear (page 501)

squat (skwot) *v.* to crouch or sit with the knees bent and drawn close to the body (page 503)

theory (thər'·ē) *n.* an opinion based on some evidence but not proved (page 504)

boast (bōst) *n.* a statement in which one brags (page 505)

registered (re'·jə·stərd) *v.* past tense of **register:** to officially record (page 506)

investment (in·vest'·mənt) *adj.* using money to buy something that will make more money (page 507)

raggedy (rag'·i·dē) *adj.* torn or worn-out (page 508)

Practice **Tell whether the boldfaced definition that is given for the underlined word in each sentence below is correct. Circle *Yes* or *No*.**

1. Luis <u>registered</u> his boat as soon as he bought it.
   officially recorded for protection.............................(Yes)   No

2. My sister finally threw away her <u>raggedy</u> doll.
   worn-out...(Yes)   No

3. My grandparents are <u>immigrants</u> from China. **a group of families descended from the same ancestor**............Yes   (No)

4. The explorers <u>rationed</u> their food supply.
   limited to fixed portions......................................(Yes)   No

5. Our <u>investment</u> in stocks was profitable.
money used to make money......................(Yes)   No

6. John tried to <u>endure</u> the long wait for his turn at the park.
to put up with......................(Yes)   No

7. His <u>theory</u> on atoms had not yet been proven wrong.
opinion proven and accepted as law........................ Yes   (No)

8. The <u>burden</u> of carrying the box up the stairs was overwhelming.
easily achieved...................................... Yes   (No)

9. I had to <u>squat</u> behind a bush to avoid being discovered.
to crouch or sit with the knees bent ....(Yes)   No

10. Jim tended to <u>boast</u> after he won his match.
to brag......................(Yes)   No

Apply   Match each word to its definition on the right.

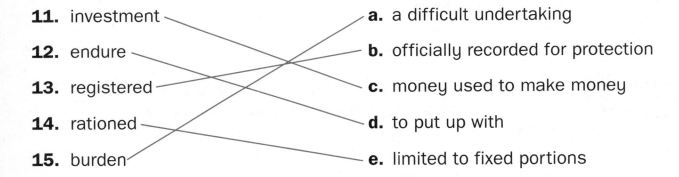

11. investment   **a.** a difficult undertaking

12. endure   **b.** officially recorded for protection

13. registered   **c.** money used to make money

14. rationed   **d.** to put up with

15. burden   **e.** limited to fixed portions

Name _____ Date _____

Sequence

When writers tell a story or explain a process, they must express the sequence in which events occur.

Sequence is indicated by time words and order words.

- Words such as *earlier, later, now, then, morning, day, evening,* and *night* indicate **time.**

- Words such as *first, second, last, following, next, after, during,* and *finally* indicate **order.**

Practice Look through "The Journal of Wong Ming-Chung." Choose one of the diary entries and summarize the sequence of events on the lines provided. Be sure to include time words and order words.

Possible Answers

Page: 500–502

Entry date: April 24

Events in sequence: First, Uncle announced his plans to prospect. Then Wong Ming-Chung said he would stay with Uncle, but Uncle told him that he had to stay with Fox. After that, Uncle left without Wong. Late that night Wong decided to go find his uncle.

_____

_____

_____

_____

Apply Think about the things you have done so far today. Make a list of those things, placing them in the proper sequence.

Possible Answer woke up, got dressed, ate breakfast, rode the bus to school, handed in my math homework

Now, write a paragraph describing your day so far. Use time words and order words to express the sequence of events in your day.

Possible Answer After I woke up this morning, I got dressed. Then I ate breakfast at the kitchen table. After that, I rode the bus to school. At school, I handed in my math homework during my first class period.

Name _____ **Date** _____

Formulating Questions and Problems

A good question or problem to investigate:

Possible Answer Was conflict between settlers and Native

Americans inevitable or could it have been avoided?

_____

_____

_____

Why this is an interesting question or problem:

Possible Answer It gives us the opportunity to examine both

sides of an issue that we do not usually get to see.

_____

_____

_____

Some other things I wonder about this question or problem:

Possible Answer Was anyone more at fault than another?

_____

_____

_____

_____

Formulating Questions and Problems (continued)

My investigation group's question or problem:

Possible Answer Was conflict between settlers and Native Americans inevitable or could it have been avoided?

_____

_____

_____

What our investigation will contribute to the rest of the class:

Possible Answer Our answers and questions will contribute to the greater class discussion of the topics.

_____

_____

_____

Some other things I wonder about this question or problem:

Possible Answer How would the United States be different if such a conflict could have been avoided?

_____

_____

_____

Name _____ **Date** _____

Poetry: Free Verse

Think

Audience: Who will read your poem?

Possible Answer my mother

Purpose: What do you want your readers to think about your poem?

Possible Answer I want my readers to think my poem is descriptive and imaginative.

Prewriting Once you have chosen a subject for your free-verse poem, use the graphic organizer below to get started. Fill in the ovals surrounding the topic with details about your subject. These details can be descriptions, thoughts, ideas, or anything else that comes to mind.

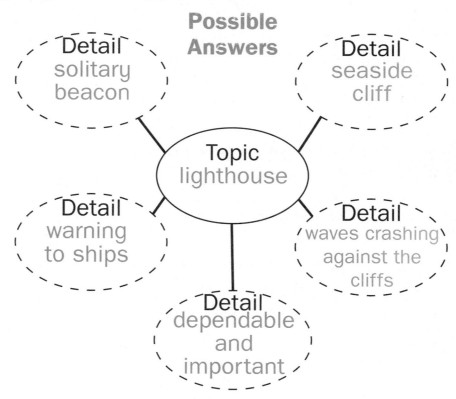

Possible Answers

Detail solitary beacon

Detail seaside cliff

Topic lighthouse

Detail warning to ships

Detail waves crashing against the cliffs

Detail dependable and important

Revising
Use this checklist to revise your poem.

☐ Did you use a thesaurus to choose vivid and precise descriptive words?

☐ Is every word and phrase in your poem necessary?

☐ Did you use figurative language to create strong images and ideas?

Editing/Proofreading
Use this checklist to correct mistakes.

☐ Have you checked your poem for misused verbs, pronouns, and modifiers?

☐ Did you use correct verb tenses?

☐ Did you use spaces and line breaks in your poem to show the reader when to pause?

☐ Did you use capitalization in a consistent way?

☐ Did you use end punctuation correctly?

Publishing
Use this checklist to prepare your poem for publication.

☐ Rewrite your poem neatly or type it on a computer to create a final copy.

☐ Practice reading your poem until you are confident you know the rhythm. Read your poem aloud to the class.

Name _____ **Date** _____

Spelling

The suffixes *-ant* and *-ent* both mean "one who" when added to words to form nouns. The suffixes mean "having the quality of" when added to words to form adjectives.

Word List

1. independent
2. excellent
3. resident
4. superintendent
5. correspondent
6. patient
7. permanent
8. convenient
9. student
10. insistent
11. important
12. observant
13. disinfectant
14. distant
15. dominant
16. relevant
17. fragrant
18. pollutant
19. abundant
20. tolerant

Practice Add the suffix *-ant* or *-ent* to the following word parts and write the resulting spelling words on the lines.

1. import ___ant___ important
2. pati ___ent___ patient
3. stud ___ent___ student
4. pollut ___ant___ pollutant
5. resid ___ent___ resident
6. conveni ___ent___ convenient
7. domin ___ant___ dominant
8. disinfect ___ant___ disinfectant
9. dist ___ant___ distant
10. correspond ___ent___ correspondent
11. fragr ___ant___ fragrant
12. independ ___ent___ independent
13. observ ___ant___ observant
14. toler ___ant___ tolerant
15. perman ___ent___ permanent

16. excell_____ent_____   excellent
17. abund_____ant_____   abundant
18. relev_____ant_____   relevant
19. insist_____ent_____   insistent
20. superintend_____ent_____   superintendent

 **Apply**   **Circle the misspelled words in the sentences and write them correctly in the spaces provided.**

21. The food was abundant and (excellant).

22. The (disinfectent) was not fragrant.

23. An (observent) student found the mistake.

24. She is the (superintendant) in a distant district.

25. The teacher praised the patient (studant).

26. Are you a (permanant) resident of this state?

27. The news correspondent traveled to (distent) lands.

28. The (independant) patient wanted to leave the hospital.

29. A certain (pollutent) is abundant in our area.

30. The (important) builder listened to the insistent residents.

excellent
disinfectant
observant
superintendent
student
permanent
distant

independent
pollutant

important

Name _____   **Date** _____

Sentence Types

- A **declarative** sentence makes a statement. It always ends with a period.

- My best friend is Reynaldo.

- An **interrogative** sentence asks a question. It ends with a question mark.

- Did you see the goal Ana scored?

- An **imperative** sentence gives a command or makes a request. It usually ends with a period.

- Please call the police.

- An **exclamatory** sentence expresses a strong feeling. It ends with an exclamation point.

- That was a yummy dessert!

Practice   **Add the correct end punctuation to these sentences.**

1. Do you know anything about Alaska?
2. The United States bought Alaska from Russia in 1867.
3. Henry Seward was the Secretary of State at that time, and he arranged to purchase Alaska for $7 million.
4. People called the territory "Seward's Folly" because they thought it cost too much money.
5. An amazing thing happened five years later.
6. The discovery of gold started a rush to Alaska.
7. Can you name two important energy sources also found there?

Apply   Label the following sentences as declarative, interrogative, imperative, or exclamatory.

8. Where is Julio taking those boxes? _interrogative_

9. Stay with Trevor until I get back from the store. _imperative_

10. While Mr. James jogged, his wife read at the library. _declarative_

11. Stop making that noise! _exclamatory_

12. Listen as I tell you about my childhood. _imperative_

13. You should eat five servings of produce each day. _declarative_

14. Does Emily know when the next train is scheduled to arrive?
interrogative

15. Please carry this message to Ms. Hampton. _imperative_

Name _____ **Date** _____

Word Relationships

Focus As you read, you will notice that many words relate to each other because they are about the same topic. These **word relationships** can give you clues about the meanings of unfamiliar words.

Practice The words in each group below are related. Determine how the words in each line are related, and write a description of the relationship on the lines below. Use a dictionary if you need help.

Possible Answers

1. deck   sail   oar   rudder

All are parts of a boat.

2. sidewalk   pathway   trail   lane

All are places to walk.

3. forest   leaves   trunk   bark

All have something to do with trees.

4. English   Spanish   French   Portuguese

All are languages.

5. roof   shingles   plywood   gutter

All are parts of a roof.

6. bat   catcher's mitt   helmet   cleats

All are pieces of sports equipment.

Apply Search the selection "Bill Pickett: Rodeo-Ridin' Cowboy." Choose five words from the selection that are related to one another. Write the words on the lines below, and then describe their relationship in column two.

Possible Answers

7. livestock
   steer
   beast
   critter
   animal

   Relationship: ⟶ words used to describe the animal Bill bulldogged

8. performing
   acts
   spectacle
   attraction
   rodeo

   Relationship: ⟶ words about entertainment

Name _____ Date _____

Selection Vocabulary

Focus

enslaved (in·slāvd') *adj.* held in slavery (page 519)

bundled (bun'·dəld) *v.* past tense of **bundle:** to tie or wrap together (page 519)

trek (trek) *n.* a long, slow journey (page 519)

prospering (pros'·pər·ing) *v.* doing extremely well (page 520)

straddled (stra'·dəld) *v.* past tense of **straddle:** to sit with one's legs on each side of an object (page 522)

rickety (ri'·ki·tē) *adj.* likely to fall or break; shaky (page 522)

challenge (chal'·ənj) *n.* a call to take part in a difficult task or contest (page 526)

lasso (la'·sō) *v.* to catch an animal using a long rope with a loop (page 527)

association (ə·sō'·sē·ā'·shən) *n.* a group of people joined together for a common purpose (page 528)

stunt (stunt) *n.* an act of skill or strength (page 528)

Practice **Circle the correct letter to answer each question below.**

1. Which is an example of the word *prospering?*
   a. a store where no one shops
   b. a store where everyone shops

2. Which is an example of a person who would use a *lasso?*
   a. someone who works in a hospital
   b. someone who works on a ranch

3. Which is an example of something that is *rickety?*
   a. a floor with holes in it
   b. a sturdy table

4. Which is an example of a *stunt?*
   a. lifting a small dog
   b. lifting five hundred pounds

5. Which is an example of something that is *bundled?*
   (a.) a stack of newspapers tied with a string
   b. a winter coat hanging in the closet

6. Which is an example of a *challenge?*
   (a.) cooking a meal for one hundred people
   b. calling a friend on the phone

7. Which is an example of an *association?*
   a. two friends going to a movie
   (b.) neighbors meeting to clean up litter every month

8. Which is an example of a *trek?*
   (a.) a cross-country trip
   b. a walk around the block

9. Which is an example of someone *enslaved?*
   (a.) a person forced to work for someone with no compensation
   b. a person who chooses to work for someone for compensation

10. Which is an example of something being *straddled?*
   (a.) riding a horse
   b. sitting on a chair

Apply   **Review the vocabulary words and definitions from *Bill Pickett: Rodeo-Ridin' Cowboy.* On a separate sheet of paper, write five sentences that each use at least one of the vocabulary words from this lesson.**

Answers will vary.

Name _____ Date _____

Fact and Opinion

 Good writers use both facts and opinions in their writing. A good reader can tell one from the other.

- **Facts** are details that can be proven true or false.

- **Opinions** are what people think. They cannot be proven true or false.

 **Skim "Bill Pickett: Rodeo-Ridin' Cowboy" for examples in which the author states facts and opinions. Write the page number, identify each example as a fact or opinion, and write the example. Be sure to find examples of both.**
Possible Answers

1. Page: _____520_____ Fact or opinion? _____Fact_____

Example: "Then the Civil War ravaged the U.S."

2. Page: _____527_____ Fact or opinion? _____Opinion_____

Example: "Soon Bill could tame broncs better than almost any other ranch hand."

3. Page: _____530_____ Fact or opinion? _____Opinion_____

Example: "They cheered the loudest of all."

4. Page: _____533_____ Fact or opinion? _____Fact_____

Example: "And in 1914 he performed in England for King George V and Queen Mary!"

Apply   **Read each sentence below and tell whether it is a fact or an opinion.**

5. Covered wagons were the best mode of transportation for pioneers.   *opinion*

6. As Americans began to explore the land out west, they found it inhabited by Native Americans.   *fact*

7. Lewis and Clark were among the first to journey west on a scientific expedition.   *fact*

8. A new life in a new land was worth the slow, steady trek pioneers made across country.   *opinion*

9. When Bill Pickett's two cousins came to visit, they bragged about their life on the trail.   *fact*

10. A cowboy's life was a good life.   *opinion*

Explorers, hunters, naturalists, cowboys, and other adventurers traveled west. Select one of these adventurers and write a paragraph about his or her travels. You may want to do some research to get factual information. Include both facts and opinions in your paragraph.

Answers will vary.

_____

_____

_____

_____

Name _____ **Date** _____

Making Conjectures

Our question or problem:

Possible Answer Why did American settlers feel the need to

migrate to the west?

_____

_____

_____

_____

Conjecture (my first theory or explanation):

Possible Answer Why did American settlers feel the need to

migrate to the west?

_____

_____

_____

_____

_____

_____

As you collect information, your conjecture will change. Return to this page to
record your new theories or explanations about your question or problem.

Establishing Investigation Needs

My group's question or problem:

Possible Answer Why did American settlers feel the need to migrate to the west?

_____

_____

_____

Knowledge Needs—Information I need to find or figure out in order to investigate the question or problem:

A. **Possible Answer** What opportunities were there in the west?

B. **Possible Answer** Were these opportunities available in the east?

C. **Possible Answer** Did the government encourage westward expansion?

D. _____

E. _____

Source	Useful?	How?
Encyclopedias	yes	for information about westward expansion
Books	yes	for information about westward expansion
Magazines		
Newspapers		
Video and Audio clips	yes	programs about western settlers
Television		
Interviews, observations	yes	learn from people whose family migrated west
Museums		
Other:		

Inquiry • _Skills Practice 2_

Name _____ Date _____

Poetry: Lyric

Think Audience: **Who** will read your lyrical poem? **Possible Answers**
<u>my teacher</u>

Purpose: **What** do you want readers to think about your poem?
<u>I want my readers to understand how I feel</u>
<u>about the poem's subject.</u>

Prewriting Lyrical poetry expresses an author's feelings about the poem's subject. Use the graphic organizer below to explore the emotions—both positive and negative—that you have about the topic you have chosen for your poem.

Possible Answers

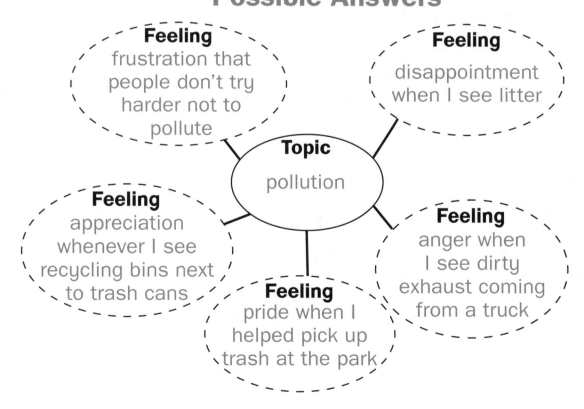

Feeling
frustration that people don't try harder not to pollute

Feeling
disappointment when I see litter

Topic
pollution

Feeling
appreciation whenever I see recycling bins next to trash cans

Feeling
pride when I helped pick up trash at the park

Feeling
anger when I see dirty exhaust coming from a truck

Revising — Use this checklist to revise your poem.

- ☐ Have you replaced bland adjectives, adverbs, and verbs with ones that are vivid and descriptive?
- ☐ If your poem rhymes, did you follow a consistent pattern throughout the poem?
- ☐ Do the words and phrases in your poem create a musical rhythm?
- ☐ Does your poem have one main focus or idea?
- ☐ Does your poem show your true feelings about the topic?

Editing/Proofreading — Use the following checklist to correct mistakes.

- ☐ Did you use commas correctly throughout your poem?
- ☐ Does your poem have any misspelled homophones?
- ☐ Did you use a consistent method for capitalization and punctuation throughout your poem?
- ☐ Have you checked for misused verbs, pronouns, or modifiers?
- ☐ Have you used standard proofreading marks to edit misspelled homophones?

Publishing — Use this checklist to prepare your poem for publication.

- ☐ Rewrite your poem neatly or type it on a computer to create a final copy.
- ☐ Add illustrations to your poem, or create a collage about your poem's topic.
- ☐ Present your poem by reading it aloud to the class or adding it to a class anthology.

Name _____ Date _____

Spelling

Focus

• **Compound words** consist of two smaller words that have been combined to form one larger word. These two words keep the same spelling in the compound word.

• **Homographs** are words that are spelled the same, but have different meanings, different word origins, and sometimes, different pronunciations.

Practice The following spelling words are missing one of their base words. Write the whole compound words on the lines.

1. camp _ground_   campground
2. _over_ head   overhead
3. news _stand_   newsstand
4. sun _light_   sunlight
5. spring _time_   springtime
6. _blue_ bonnet   bluebonnet
7. _stock_ yards   stockyards
8. bare _foot_   barefoot
9. mean _while_   meanwhile
10. _motor_ cycle   motorcycle

Word List
1. bluebonnet
2. stockyards
3. newsstand
4. sunlight
5. campground
6. meanwhile
7. motorcycle
8. springtime
9. barefoot
10. overhead
11. invalid
12. launch
13. minute
14. school
15. spruce
16. capital
17. refuse
18. compound
19. reserved
20. cardinal

On the line, write the homograph from the spelling list after its brief definition.

11. to say no   refuse

12. person who is disabled   invalid

13. to put in motion   launch

14. very small   minute

15. group of fish   school

16. to make neat or trim   spruce

17. money or assets   capital

18. enclosed area with buildings   compound

19. of greatest importance   cardinal

20. quiet or shy   reserved

Apply **On the line, write the spelling word from the list that contains one of the base words in the following compound words**

21. flashlight   sunlight

22. headache   overhead

23. tricycle   motorcycle

24. awhile   meanwhile

25. blueberry   bluebonnet

26. threadbare   barefoot

27. campsite   campground

28. anytime   springtime

29. backyards   stockyards

30. newspaper   newsstand

Name _____   Date _____

Colons and Semicolons

Focus
- **Colons** (:) are used to introduce lists, to separate the minutes and hours of a precise time, and at the end of a business letter's salutation.

- **Semicolons** (;) are used to join independent clauses in a sentence and to help separate clauses joined by some adverbs. Use a semicolon when conjunctions like *and* or *but* are not used.

Practice Each sentence below contains a colon or a semicolon. If the correct punctuation mark was used, write *C* in the blank. If the incorrect punctuation mark was used, write *I* in the blank.

1. ___I___ My brother thought I took his favorite book: he was wrong.

2. ___C___ Hannah's day always consists of the following meals: breakfast, lunch, and dinner.

3. ___I___ To whom it may concern;

4. ___I___ Our match starts at exactly 10;15.

5. ___C___ Earthquakes are caused by movement deep underground; however, they can still be felt at the surface.

6. ___I___ Aunt Millie always brings these things when she visits; baked goods, a couple of books, and a big smile.

7. ___C___ Juan just returned from Alaska; he's heading to Montana next.

8. ___C___ Every Wednesday at 4:00 I have dance lessons.

Apply Add colons and/or semicolons where they are needed in the following sentences.

9. Marcus searched for blueberries on his hike; he did not find any.

10. The race began at 9:15; my family was there watching from the sidelines.

11. Please try to bring one of the following items: a tablecloth, eating utensils, napkins, or cleaning supplies.

12. Shawna thought she had caught a lightning bug; when she opened her hand, it was gone.

13. Earth has four oceans: the Pacific, the Atlantic, the Indian, and the Arctic.

14. Tell Li to memorize the code; she'll get locked out if she doesn't remember it.

15. Go to the fridge and grab the milk, three eggs, and some cheese; we're going to make an omelet.

16. Last night at 7:30, Kyle received a call from overseas; however, it was a wrong number.

Name _____   Date _____

Synonyms and Antonyms

Focus

- **Synonyms** are words with the same, or nearly the same, meaning. For example, *giant, huge,* and *massive* are all synonyms.

- **Antonyms** are words with opposite or nearly opposite meanings. An antonym for *empty* is *full,* and an antonym for *dull* is *exciting.*

Practice

The first word of each pair below is from "Ghost Towns of the American West." Write **S** on the line if the second word is a synonym. Write **A** on the line if it is an antonym.

1. __S__ communities   neighborhoods

2. __S__ lonely   isolated

3. __A__ vanished   appeared

4. __A__ general   specific

5. __S__ fragile   delicate

6. __S__ rubbish   garbage

7. __A__ vacant   occupied

8. __S__ cheerful   upbeat

9. __S__ surrounded   enclosed

10. __S__ longing   hoping

Apply For each word below, write an antonym on the first line and a synonym on the second line. Use a dictionary and thesaurus if you need help.

Possible Answers

11. suspicious

Antonym: _____ trusting _____ Synonym: _____ wary _____

12. removed

Antonym: _____ added _____ Synonym: subtracted

13. fake

Antonym: _____ genuine _____ Synonym: artificial

14. entire

Antonym: _____ partial _____ Synonym: complete

15. professional

Antonym: _____ amateur _____ Synonym: _____ expert _____

16. nervous

Antonym: _____ calm _____ Synonym: _____ jumpy _____

17. created

Antonym: _____ destroyed _____ Synonym: _____ made _____

18. foreign

Antonym: _____ domestic _____ Synonym: _____ exotic _____

Name _____ **Date** _____

Selection Vocabulary

Focus

longed (longd) *v.* past tense of **long**: to want very much; yearn (page 548)

evidence (e' · və · dəns) *n.* proof of something (page 548)

tattered (tat' · ərd) *adj.* torn into shreds (page 549)

trough (trôf) *n.* a long narrow container that holds water or food for animals (page 549)

territory (ter' · i · tôr' · ē) *n.* a large area or region of land (page 549)

centuries (sen' · chə · rēz) *n.* plural of **century**: a period of one hundred years (page 549)

minerals (min' · ər · əlz) *n.* plural of **mineral**: a substance found in nature that is not an animal or plant. Salt, coal, and gold are minerals. (page 550)

prosperity (pros · per' · i · tē) *n.* success, wealth, or good fortune (page 550)

traces (trās' · ez) *n.* plural of **trace**: a small bit or sign left behind showing that something was there (page 551)

inhabitants (in · ha' · bə · tənts) *n.* plural of **inhabitant**: a person or animal that lives in a place (page 557)

Practice Circle the letter of the word that correctly completes each sentence.

1. The only _____ of the party were a few crumbs and empty cups sitting on the table.

   a. minerals **(b.)** traces **c.** inhabitants

2. The bottom edge of the curtain was _____ where the cat had been playing with it.

   a. longed **b.** traces **(c.)** tattered

3. The Abu-Jabars have lived in the _____ since the 1930s.

   a. inhabitants **(b.)** territory **c.** prosperity

4. The mining company owns all the _____ that they dig out of the mountain.

    a. minerals   **b.** evidence   **c.** trough

5. For _____, kings and queens ruled much of the world.

    a. prosperity   **b.** inhabitants   **c.** centuries

6. A _____ filled with water ran along one entire side of the barn.

    a. minerals   **b.** trough   **c.** longed

7. The detective quickly saw that all the _____ was fake.

    a. traces   **b.** minerals   **c.** evidence

8. The McKenzies' _____ came from owning a store.

    a. prosperity   **b.** minerals   **c.** territory

9. The _____ of the rain forest know how to use the land's resources.

    a. inhabitants   **b.** territory   **c.** traces

10. After several weeks away from home, Sara _____ to see her family.

    a. prosperity   **b.** traces   **c.** longed

Apply   **Write the vocabulary word that best matches the underlined word or phrase in the sentences below.**

11. A dozen hogs lined up to eat at the <u>long, narrow container</u> filled with grain.

    trough

12. <u>For hundreds of years</u> the castle has stood towering over the valley.

    centuries

13. During the first week, I <u>wanted</u> to be back at my old school.

    longed

14. The only way to <u>success</u> is through hard work.   prosperity

Name _____ Date _____

Poetry: Quatrain

**Think**

Audience: Who will read your quatrain? **Possible Answers**

a friend _____

Purpose: What do you want your readers to think about your quatrain?

I want my audience to think I used sensory details well in my poem.

Prewriting

Including sensory details in your poem will make its images more vivid and complex. Use this graphic organizer to plan your quatrain.

Possible Answers

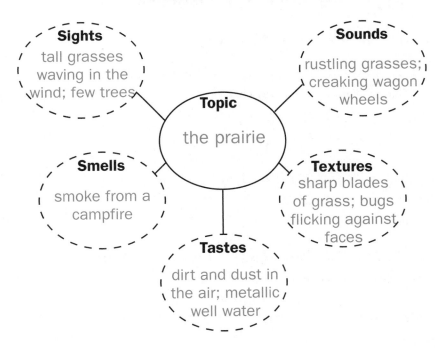

Revising
Use this checklist to revise your quatrain.

- ☐ Do you use a correct rhyming pattern for your quatrain?

- ☐ Have you used a thesaurus or rhyming dictionary to choose unique and descriptive words?

- ☐ Do your words and sensory details convey the mood of your poem?

- ☐ Does your poem have a consistent rhyming pattern?

- ☐ Do the words, phrases, and punctuation create a noticeable rhythm?

Editing/Proofreading
Use the following checklist to correct mistakes.

- ☐ Does your poem have any spelling errors?

- ☐ Did you use a consistent method for capitalization and punctuation throughout your poem?

- ☐ Have you correctly used one or more of the possible rhyming patterns?

- ☐ Have you correctly used participial phrases, transition words, and commas?

Publishing
Use this checklist to prepare your poem for publication.

- ☐ Rewrite your poem neatly, or type it on a computer to create a final copy.

- ☐ Use paste-up to add graphics representing the sensory details in your poem.

- ☐ Present your poem by reading it aloud to the class, adding it to a class anthology, or entering it in a poetry contest.

Name _____ **Date** _____

Spelling

Focus

• **Synonyms** are words with the same, or nearly the same, meaning. Use synonyms to help you remember the meaning of a new word.

• A **base word family** is a family of words that share a base word. When you know the meaning of a base word, you can begin to determine the meanings of the other words in the base word family.

Word List

1. expansion
2. growth
3. opportunity
4. chance
5. fortune
6. wealth
7. gratitude
8. appreciation
9. petite
10. undersized
11. special
12. specialty
13. especially
14. include
15. inclusive
16. inclusion
17. command
18. commander
19. commandeer
20. commanding

Practice

On the lines, write word pairs from the word list that are synonyms. Use a thesaurus or dictionary if you need help. **Possible Answers**

1. expansion
2. growth
3. opportunity
4. chance
5. fortune
6. wealth
7. gratitude
8. appreciation
9. petite
10. undersized

Complete each base word and write the resulting spelling word on the line.

11. ___spec___ial   special
12. ___in___clude   include
13. ___com___mand   command

On the line, write the base word in each spelling word on the line.

14. commandeer command   18. inclusion include

15. inclusive include   19. commanding command

16. especially special   20. specialty special

17. commander command

Apply For each word, list the spelling words that are synonyms. **Possible Answers**

enlargement

1. expansion

2. growth

thanks

3. gratitude

4. appreciation

riches

5. fortune

6. wealth

occasion

7. chance

8. opportunity

Correct each underlined word and write it on the line. If the word is already correct, write correct.

9. That movie was <u>espeshully</u> good.

especially

10. Do not forget to <u>include</u> a tip.

correct

11. Apple pie is my aunt's <u>speshialty</u>.

specialty

12. They voted on his <u>incloosion</u> in their club.

inclusion

13. I <u>comand</u> you to open the door.

command

14. The ship's <u>comander</u> fell sick.

commander

Name _____ **Date** _____

Transition Words

Focus **Transition words** link sentences and paragraphs to each other. They help ideas flow smoothly. Transition words make writing clearer, more accurate, and help the reader move smoothly from one idea to another.

- Transition words show time: *yesterday, the day before yesterday, this morning, today, tomorrow, tonight, this afternoon, this moment.*

- Transition words show order of occurrence: *earlier, about, as soon as, soon, finally, when, meanwhile, until, later, next, now, then, finally, last.*

- Transition words show contrast: *although, but, even, though, however, on the other hand, otherwise, still, while, yet, in contrast.*

- Use transition words to compare two things: *also, too, both, in the same way, just as, likewise, like, similarly.*

- Transition words signal additional information: *additionally, again, along with, also, and, another, besides, finally, for example, further, moreover.*

- Transition words introduce a conclusion or a summary: *as a result, finally, in conclusion, in summary, last, lastly, therefore.*

Practice **Transition words may be used for more than one purpose in a paragraph. Circle the transition words used below.**

1. (Both) Tiana and Maya like swimming, (but) Maya likes to swim freestyle (and) Tiana prefers the butterfly stroke. (Both) (also) swim the backstroke. (Yesterday) they practiced all three strokes for the meet (today.) (This morning) they woke up (early,) had a good breakfast, and did stretching exercises. (This afternoon) they will each swim in two events.

 **Apply** — Cross out the two transition words *least* likely to be used for each writing assignment.

2. Writing Assignment   **Transition Words**

The end of a persuasive report   *in conclusion, ~~yesterday,~~ therefore, finally, ~~underneath~~*

A description of a waterfall   *~~in summary,~~ above, at the bottom, ~~moreover,~~ under*

A contrast of two books   *~~both,~~ but, however, ~~likewise,~~ on the other hand*

Possible Answers

3. Use transition words that show location to describe a school bus.

The school bus is parked next to the curb.

4. Use transition words that signal additional information to describe a school policy.

Bikes must be kept outside. Additionally, skateboards cannot be ridden in the halls.

5. Use transition words that compare and contrast to describe two different pets.

My dog, Sam, has white fur, but my cat, Lana, is gray.

6. Use transition words to introduce the concluding paragraph for either an imaginary school report or for one you wrote earlier this year.

In conclusion, this book was my favorite so far this year.

Name _____ Date _____

Language/Word Structure and the Suffix *-ic*

Focus

Understanding **word structure** can help you discover the meanings of words. Identifying the individual parts of a word's structure can help you determine the word's meaning.

• The suffix **-ic** means "of," "relating to," or "possessing the characteristics of." It usually forms adjectives.

Practice

Divide each of the following words into base words, prefixes, suffixes, and other inflectional endings. Circle each word that contains the suffix *-ic* and write its definition on the line.

1. discovered dis + cover + ed

_____

2. (unpoetic) un + poet + ic

_____

3. (nonmetallic) non + metall + ic

_____

4. (unrealistic) un + realist + ic

_____

5. exactly exact + ly

_____

 Combine each base word below with at least two word parts from the box to create five new words. Then use each new word correctly in a sentence. Possible Answers

ed	tion	en	dis	non	ly
less	pre	mis	ing	in	able

6. Base word: order   New word: <u>preordering</u>

Sentence: <u>I am preordering tickets to the first football game this year.</u>

7. Base word: stop   New word: <u>nonstop</u>

Sentence: <u>There will be a nonstop showing of all Spiderman movies this Saturday.</u>

8. Base word: use   New word: <u>uselessly</u>

Sentence: <u>Our snow shovel has leaned uselessly against the garage wall since we moved south.</u>

9. Base word: joy   New word: <u>enjoyable</u>

Sentence: <u>The last movie I saw was very enjoyable.</u>

10. Base word: large   New word: <u>enlarged</u>

Sentence: <u>We enlarged the photo on the computer.</u>

Name _____ **Date** _____

Selection Vocabulary

Focus

regard (re·gärd')
n. thought or care
(page 566)

merciful (mûr'·si·fəl) *adj.* kind or
forgiving (page 566)

predict (pri'·dikt) *v.* to tell
beforehand (page 567)

accurate (ak'·yər·it) *adj.* correct;
exact (page 567)

drought (drout) *n.* a period of time
when there is very little rain or no
rain at all (page 571)

prairie (prâ'·rē) *n.* a large area
of level or rolling land with grass
and few or no trees (page 573)

desperately (des'·pə·rət·lē)
adv. hopelessly (page 573)

sowing (sō'·ing) *v.* planting
(page 575)

heaved (hēvd) *v.* past tense of
heave: to make a sound with a
lot of effort or strain (page 575)

dispositions (dis'·pə·zi'·shənz)
n. plural of **disposition:** a natural
way of acting; mood (page 576)

Practice Write the word from the word box that matches each definition below.

1. _desperately_ hopelessly

2. _merciful_ kind or forgiving

3. _prairie_ a large area of level or rolling land with grass and few or no trees

4. _heaved_ make a sound with a lot of effort or strain

5. _regard_ thought or care

6. _drought_ dry weather that lasts a long time

7. _sowing_ planting

8. _dispositions_ natural ways of acting

9. _____predict_____ to tell beforehand

10. _____accurate_____ correct; exact

Circle the word in parentheses that best fits each sentence.

11. Reno was (sowing/predict) seeds in the pumpkin patch.

12. She showed no (regard/dispositions) for the hard work of her teammates.

13. My mother is usually (merciful/accurate) when I do something wrong.

14. The crops are dying because of the (drought/prairie).

15. Dawn is (rowdy/desperately) trying to finish her homework before bedtime.

16. The wind moves quickly across the (drought/prairie).

17. They hoped that the weather forecast was (accurate/merciful).

18. Everyone likes my brothers because they have cheerful (legends/dispositions).

Name _____ **Date** _____

Cause and Effect

Most stories revolve around several cause-and-effect relationships. Recognizing these relationships can help readers better understand the story.

A **cause** is why something happened.

An **effect** is what happened.

When one event causes another to happen, the events have a cause-and-effect relationship.

- A **cause** is the reason that an event happens.

- An **effect** is the result of the cause.

- Writers use words such as *because, since, therefore,* and *so* to show the reader that a cause-and-effect relationship has taken place.

Look through "McBroom the Rainmaker" and identify four effects on animals caused by the drought. Possible Answers

Effect: Dogs fought over a bone just for the moisture in it.

Effect: The hens laid fried eggs.

Effect: The cow gave powdered milk.

Effect: The catfish dried up.

Apply Read the sentences below and identify the cause and effect in each one.

1. We spent our bus money at the mall, so we had to walk home.

Effect: We had to walk home.

Cause: We spent our bus money at the mall.

2. My dad gave me five dollars because I washed the car.

Effect: My dad gave me five dollars.

Cause: I washed the car.

3. I stayed home from school because I was sick.

Effect: I stayed home from school.

Cause: I was sick.

4. I slipped on the ice and broke my ankle.

Effect: I broke my ankle.

Cause: I slipped on the ice.

5. My dog started barking when he heard the doorbell ring.

Effect: The dog started barking.

Cause: The dog heard the doorbell ring.

On a separate sheet of paper, write a paragraph that includes several cause-and-effect relationships. You might use one of the sentences above as the basis of your paragraph.

Answers will vary.

Comprehension Skill • *Skills Practice 2*

Name _____   **Date** _____

Tall Tale

Think   **Audience: Who** will read your tall tale? **Possible Answers**
first graders

Purpose: What is your purpose for writing a tall tale?
I want my readers to think the story is funny and entertaining.

Prewriting   **Use this graphic organizer to plan your tall tale.**

Possible Answers

Title
Speedy McLean, Slow Down!

Who
Speedy McLean, Slomo Joe, residents of Slow Junction

Where
Slow Junction

When
in the Old West

Key Events
- Speedy arrives in town
- Speedy becomes friends with Slomo Joe
- Speedy gets a job at a barbershop but gives bad haircuts because he works too fast
- Speedy gets a job at a restaurant but clears the plates before people finish eating

Conflict
Speedy does everything quickly, often too quickly, and this bothers the citizens of Slow Junction.

Resolution
The residents of Slow Junction promise to speed up a little while Speedy promises to try taking his time.

Revising Use this checklist to revise your draft.

☐ Have you used transitional phrases to clarify events and tighten plot?

☐ Have you included enough sensory details to establish mood and make your characters come alive on the page?

☐ Does your plot have a problem, rising action, and a climax?

☐ Have you consistently used a point of view for your story?

☐ Have you used hyperbole and exaggeration?

☐ Have you deleted repetitious ideas and combined sentences?

Editing/Proofreading Use this checklist to edit your draft.

☐ Have you correctly used appositives, verb tense, and participial phrases?

☐ Are the names you have invented for people and places humorous and silly?

☐ Have you capitalized and spelled the names of people and places consistently throughout your story?

☐ Have you used transition words to help your story flow?

Publishing Use this checklist to publish your draft.

☐ Neatly type your tall tale.

☐ Illustrate your tall tale and share it with others.

Name _____ **Date** _____

Spelling

Focus

• Some words end in the suffix **-ic**, which means "of," "relating to," or "possessing the characteristics of."

• When adding an ending that begins with a vowel, such as *-er, -es,* or *-ed,* to a word ending in a consonant and a *y,* change the *y* to an *i.* If a word ends with a vowel and a *y,* just add the ending. Do not change the *y* to an *i* if the ending is *-ing.*

Word List
1. metallic
2. poetic
3. realistic
4. historic
5. classic
6. artistic
7. basic
8. dramatic
9. oceanic
10. patriotic
11. heavy
12. heavier
13. butterfly
14. butterflies
15. supply
16. supplies
17. worry
18. worried
19. mercy
20. merciful

Practice **Add the suffix -ic to the following base words.**

1. artist + -ic = artistic
2. patriot + -ic = patriotic
3. metal + -ic = metallic
4. class + -ic = classic
5. drama + -ic = dramatic
6. realist + -ic = realistic
7. base + -ic = basic
8. poet + -ic = poetic
9. ocean + -ic = oceanic
10. history + -ic = historic

Remove the suffixes from the following words and write the resulting spelling words on the lines.

11. worried _worry_

12. merciful _mercy_

13. supplies _supply_

14. butterflies _butterfly_

15. heavier _heavy_

Add the endings to the following base words and write the resulting spelling words on the lines.

16. butterfly + -es = _butterflies_

17. worry + -ed = _worried_

18. supply + -es = _supplies_

19. mercy + -ful = _merciful_

20. heavy + -er = _heavier_

Apply Correct the spelling of each underlined word that is a part of a base word family and write it on the line. If the word is already correct, write correct.

21. The action scenes were very <u>reelistic</u>. _realistic_

22. That rock looks almost <u>muhtallic</u>. _metallic_

23. She has always been <u>artistic</u>. _correct_

24. The <u>osheeanic</u> breeze feels good. _oceanic_

25. Flying the flag is <u>patriahtic</u>. _patriotic_

26. This math is very <u>baseic</u>. _basic_

Name _____ Date _____

Appositives and Participial Phrases

Focus Appositives and participial phrases are similar to adjectives because they modify nouns or pronouns.

- An **appositive** is a noun that modifies or renames another noun or pronoun.

  My school, **DuBois Elementary,** is a fun place to learn.

- An **appositive phrase** consists of an appositive and the words that modify it.

  Uncle Chris went to France, **a country in Europe,** to study art.

- A **participial phrase** includes a verb and other words in the phrase that modify a noun or pronoun.

  The bike, **leaning quietly against the wall,** reflected sunlight onto the ground.

Practice Circle each appositive and appositive phrase in the following sentences. Underline each participial phrase.

1. That old house standing at the corner of Broad and Main will be torn down.

2. The Old West, that place of legends and adventure, has been the setting for many movies.

3. Ice cream, a popular treat throughout the world, was invented thousands of years ago.

4. Anything piled in that box can be taken to the resale shop located downtown.

5. Our teacher, Ms. Reynolds, has an aquarium filled with tropical fish.

 **Add an appositive, an appositive phrase, or a participial phrase to each sentence below.**

Example: The street was filled with cars.
The street, on which I live, was filled with cars. **Possible Answers**

6. Your brother is known around school for his talent at basketball.

Your brother, Craig, is known around school for his talent at basketball.

7. Theo walked out the library's front door.

Theo, carrying a huge stack of books, walked out the library's front door.

8. The pizza had tomato sauce, cheese, and pepperoni.

The pizza had tomato sauce, cheese, and pepperoni, my favorite topping.

9. Those paintbrushes need to be cleaned.

Those paintbrushes, a gift from my dad, need to be cleaned.

10. Our trip to New York was canceled.

Our trip to New York, planned months in advance, was canceled.

Name _____ Date _____

Prefix *im-*, Synonyms, and Antonyms

Focus

The prefix **im-** means "not." When *im-* is added to the beginning of a word, it creates an antonym of the base word. For example, the word *perfect* becomes *imperfect*.

- **Synonyms** are words with the same, or nearly the same, meaning. For example, *giant, huge,* and *massive* are all synonyms.

- **Antonyms** are words that mean with opposite, or nearly opposite, meanings. An antonym for *empty* is *full* and an antonym for *dull* is *exciting*.

Practice A

Remember the prefix *in-* also means "not." You must be careful to choose the correct prefix when creating a word's antonym. For each word below, circle its correctly formed antonym.

1. Antonym for *possible:*   inpossible   (impossible)

2. Antonym for *correct:*   (incorrect)   imcorrect

3. Antonym for *mature:*   inmature   (immature)

4. Antonym for *patiently:*   inpatiently   (impatiently)

5. Antonym for *balance:*   inbalance   (imbalance)

6. Antonym for *capable:*   (incapable)   imcapable

7. Antonym for *proper:*   inproper   (improper)

8. Antonym for *experienced:*   (inexperienced)   imexperienced

9. Antonym for *frequent:*   (infrequent)   imfrequent

10. Antonym for *polite:*   inpolite   (impolite)

Practice B

Look at the word pairs listed. Write an *S* next to the word pair if they are synonyms and an *A* next to the pair if they are antonyms.

11. memorial   monument   _____S_____

12. design   plan   _____S_____

13. friend   enemy   _____A_____

14. forward   backward   _____A_____

15. thankful   grateful   _____S_____

Apply

Not every word that begins with *im-* uses it as a prefix meaning "not." Read the words below. If the word uses *im-* as a prefix, write its base word on the line. If the word does not use *im-* as a prefix, then circle the word. Use a dictionary if you need help.

16. imperfect   Base word: ___perfect___

17. (imply)   Base word: _____

18. immobile   Base word: ___mobile___

19. (imitation)   Base word: _____

20. (imagination)   Base word: _____

Name _____ Date _____

Selection Vocabulary

Focus

equator (i • kwā' • tər) *n.* the imaginary line that circles Earth's center halfway between the North and South Poles (page 594)

horrified (hor' • ə • fīd) *v.* past tense of **horrify**: to cause a feeling of great fear and dread (page 595)

tropics (trop' • iks) *n.* a region of Earth that is near the equator (page 595)

biologist (bī • o' • lə • jəst) *n.* a person who studies the way in which plants and animals and other living things live and grow, and where they are found (page 596)

species (spē' • sēz) *n.* a group of animals or plants that have many characteristics in common (page 598)

macaw (mə • kô') *n.* a long-tailed parrot (page 598)

donations (dō • nā' • shənz) *n.* plural of **donation**: a gift or contribution (page 601)

designed (di • zīnd') *v.* past tense of **design**: to create (page 602)

grateful (grāt' • fəl) *adj.* full of thanks for a favor (page 603)

monument (mon' • yə •mənt) *n.* a building or statue that is made to honor a person or event (page 605)

Practice   Write *T* in the blank if the sentence for the vocabulary word is correct. Write *F* if the sentence is false. For every *F* answer, write the vocabulary word that fits the definition.

1. *Donations* are gifts. ___T_____

2. The *species* is a region of Earth near the equator. ___F____

   ____tropics_____

3. When a building is *designed,* it is created. ___T_____

4. A *biologist* is something that serves to honor or keep alive a memory. __F__ monument

5. The *tropics* is the imaginary line that circles Earth's center. __F__ equator

6. Someone who is *grateful* is thankful. __T__ _____

7. A *macaw* is a type of bird. __T__ _____

8. A person who is *horrified* has a great sense of fear and dread. __T__ _____

9. A *monument* is a person who studies plant and animal life. __F__ biologist

10. A *species* is a group of animals or plants that have many characteristics in common. __T__ _____

 **Apply**   **Circle the word in parentheses that best fits each sentence below.**

11. The people were ((horrified)/designed) by the tornado.

12. A large stone (species/(monument)) stands in city hall.

13. The imaginary line that divides Earth in half is called the (biologist/(equator)).

14. Do you know how many ((species)/tropics) of snakes live in the Amazon River?

15. Our school accepted (species/(donations)) of new books.

Name _____ Date _____

Author's Purpose

Focus The author's reason for writing a story is called the **author's purpose.**

- The author's purpose can be to inform, explain, entertain, or persuade. An author can have more than one purpose for writing.
- The author's purpose affects the details, descriptions, pictures, and dialogue that are included in a story.

Practice Reread "Founders of the Children's Rain Forest" and then answer the following questions.

1. What do you think the author's main purpose or purposes were for writing this selection?

Possible Answer to inform or to explain

2. What makes you think this was the purpose?

Possible Answer The selection gives a lot of information about the rain forest, and it provides a detailed explanation of how the children founded the Children's Rain Forest.

3. How successful do you think the author was in this purpose?

Possible Answer The author was very successful.

Read the following paragraphs and write the author's purpose for each.

4. The story "Alice in Wonderland" was originally written by Lewis Carroll as a gift for a young child named Alice. The story included his own illustrations. These were very different from any of the illustrations that were done later when he expanded the story into a book-length version.

   Author's purpose: _____ to inform _____

5. I invented a new game. You need four bases, in-line skates for all players, a soccer ball, and a bat. First, set up the bases as you would in baseball—first, second, third, and home. Then, have a pitcher throw the soccer ball to the batter. The batter tries to hit the ball with the bat. As in baseball, the batter has three strikes before he or she is out. If the batter is successful, he or she skates around the bases. Doesn't it sound like fun?

   Author's purpose: _____ to explain _____

Apply Take some factual information that you know or have heard in the news and use it to write an opening paragraph for an entertaining story.

Answers will vary.

_____

_____

_____

_____

_____

Name _____ Date _____

Record Concept Information

As I read the selection, this is what I added to my understanding of the call of duty.

- "Founders of the Children's Rain Forest" by Phillip Hoose

  Possible Answer I learned that everyone can make a difference if they work together and that even a place as far away as the rain forests in Monteverde is worth me trying to help save.

- "Jason and the Golden Fleece" by Geraldine McCaughrean

  Possible Answer I learned that Jason's journey and experiences with fighting off Harpies and slaying a dragon represent a spiritual or personal journey rather than a real one. He succeeded in completing

- "The Quest for Healing" by Philip Ardagh   his duty of getting the fleece.

  Possible Answer I learned that Native Americans believe all things— plants, animals, and people—have the same spirit inside. Because they share the same spirit, it is an obligation not to be wasteful or greedy.

- "The White Spider's Gift" by Jaime Turner

  Possible Answer I learned that it is important to help others. This play from Paraguay reminds me of the story of the Good Samaritan.

- "The Story of Annie Sullivan: Helen Keller's Teacher" by Bernice Selden

  Possible Answer I learned that Annie had many struggles with Helen trying to teach her. Annie was dedicated and finally was able to teach Helen. It is important not to give up even when it seems like things are very difficult.

Knowledge about the Call of Duty

- This is what I know about the call of duty before reading the unit.

  Possible Answer I have an uncle in the military and he
  said it as his duty to serve his country. Duty means taking
  responsibility.

  _____

  _____

  _____

- These are some things about the call of duty that I would like to talk about and understand better.

  Possible Answer Why do people feel a need to serve their
  country in the military? Are there other ways to serve one's
  country? What is my obligation to others?

  _____

  _____

  _____

Reminder: I should read this page again when I get to the end of the unit to see how much my ideas about the call of duty have changed.

Name _____ **Date** _____

Ideas about the Call of Duty

Of the ideas discussed in class about the call of duty, these are the ones I found most interesting.

Possible Answer Duty is many things to many different

people. But it does have the common element of loyalty,

honesty, and perseverance.

_____

_____

_____

_____

_____

_____

_____

_____

_____

_____

_____

_____

_____

_____

Ideas about the Call of Duty (continued)

Write down the ideas you found most interesting about the selection "Founders of the Children's Rain Forest." Discuss your ideas with the class.

Possible Answer Despite the young age of these students, they were never afraid or intimidated by the enormity of their project. This was largely because they thought that the little they could do was enough. That turned into an inspiration to others.

Name _____ Date _____

Writing a Personal Letter Via the Web

Think   **Audience: Who** will read your personal letter?

Possible Answer my cousin

Purpose: What do you want to say in your personal letter?

Possible Answer I want to tell my cousin about a book I just read.

Prewriting   **Personal letters are less formal than business letters, but they should still be polite and well written. The amount of detail you will need to include depends on how much your audience already knows about the topic. Use the following lines to determine which details should be included in your letter.**

Possible Answers

What is the topic of your personal letter?

Ramona's World by Beverly Cleary

What does your audience already know about the topic?

My cousin has read some of the other Ramona books. Her

favorite book is *The Mouse and the Motorcycle,* also by

Beverly Cleary.

What do you need to tell your audience about the topic?

I will tell my cousin about characters other than Ramona that

appear in the book. I will also tell her some of the plot, but not

the ending.

Revising
Use this checklist to revise your personal letter.

- ☐ Does your letter contain a salutation, body, closing, and your name?
- ☐ Did you leave out the details that your audience would have already known?
- ☐ Have you deleted and consolidated to eliminate wordiness?
- ☐ Have you checked all the helping verbs in your sentences to be sure they are necessary?
- ☐ Is the tone of your letter friendly and not too formal?

Editing/Proofreading
Use this checklist to make corrections.

- ☐ Is your personal letter formatted correctly?
- ☐ Did you check all capitalization, spelling, and punctuation?
- ☐ Did you correctly use nouns, verbs, adjectives, and adverbs?
- ☐ Have you entered the correct e-mail address into the address bar?

Publishing
Use this checklist to publish your personal letter.

- ☐ If your letter was written in a word-processing program, attach it to an e-mail message.
- ☐ Click the send button.

Name _____ Date _____

Spelling

Focus
- **Root words** were formed from words of other languages, such as Greek and Latin. Here are some roots in the spelling words and their meanings:
  bio = "life" **graph** = "write" **auto** = "self"
  dem = "people" **crat** = "person of power; ruler"
- The prefix **im-** usually means "not."

Word List
1. biography
2. biologist
3. biosphere
4. biorhythm
5. democracy
6. aristocrat
7. autocrat
8. democratic
9. aristocratic
10. autocratic
11. impossible
12. impolite
13. impatient
14. immature
15. impartial
16. impassable
17. impermanent
18. impersonal
19. impractical
20. imperfect

Practice Fill in the missing root and write the spelling word that is formed.

dem
1. dem ocracy   democracy
2. dem ocratic   democratic

bio
3. bio logist   biologist
4. bio graphy   biography
5. bio rhythm   biorhythm
6. bio sphere   biosphere

auto
7. auto crat   autocrat
8. auto cratic   autocratic

crat
9. aristo crat   aristocrat
10. aristo crat ic   aristocratic

Add the prefix *im-* to the following base words to form spelling words. Write the spelling words on the lines.

11. partial   impartial

12. personal   impersonal

13. possible   impossible

14. permanent   impermanent

15. polite   impolite

16. patient   impatient

17. mature   immature

18. passable   impassable

19. perfect   imperfect

20. practical   impractical

 **Apply** On the line, write the spelling word that is represented by the following combinations.

21. "life" + logist   biologist

22. "people" + ocracy   democracy

23. "self" + "ruler"   autocrat

24. "life" + sphere   biosphere

25. "people" + "ruler" + ic   democratic

Use the phrase to help you determine the spelling word that fits the description best, and write the word on the line.

26. not perfect   imperfect

27. not wanting to wait   impatient

28. not able to be passed   impassable

29. not old   immature

30. not polite   impolite

Name _____ Date _____

Helping Verbs and Linking Verbs, Subjects and Predicates

Focus

- **Helping verbs,** also known as auxiliary verbs, work with a sentence's main verb to show action.

  Constance **will** attend camp this summer.

- **Linking verbs** are state-of-being verbs that express what a subject is or is like. State-of-being verbs can also express where one is.

  That painting **is** beautiful.

- The **subject** is the part of the sentence that tells *who* or *what*.

  The students visited a nature preserve.

- The **predicate** describes or tells what the subject does.

  The students **visited a nature preserve.**

Practice A
In the sentences below, circle the linking verbs, and underline the helping verbs. Remember that a sentence might contain more than one helping verb.

1. Mr. Thompson's feet ⟨are⟩ sore from running a marathon.

2. The builders <u>will</u> chop down those trees for the new mall.

3. You <u>must</u> join us for dinner some time.

4. The pears ⟨tasted⟩ delicious on top of the ice cream.

5. By the time water reaches your house, it <u>will have</u> traveled many miles.

Practice B Circle each subject and underline each predicate in the following sentences.

6. (Denzel) was a role model to many children.

7. (Hannah) always tried to do the right thing.

8. (Samir) always cheered for his favorite team, but (he) always respected the opposing team.

9. (The dog) and (the cat) drank from the same bowl.

10. (Kathy) and (Gary) were looking forward to the celebration on Saturday.

Apply Write two sentences for each verb. Use the verb as an action verb in the first sentence and a linking verb in the second sentence.

11. **look**   Action verb:
Possible Answer I am looking for an opponent for a chess match.

Linking verb:
Possible Answer My hair looks messy today.

12. **stay**   Action verb:
Possible Answer Stay near the phone until I call.

Linking verb:
Possible Answer The sky stays cloudy for most of the winter.

Name _____ **Date** _____

Levels of Specificity and Irregular Verbs

Focus When writers want to describe something the best they can, they try not to use a general word, but a word that is more specific and paints a certain picture for the reader.

We were impressed with the entertainer who loudly announced the next act—the animals.

We were impressed with the ringmaster who loudly announced the next act—the lions.

You know that the rule for forming the past tense of most verbs is to add -ed. **Irregular verbs** do not follow this rule.

- For example, *run* and *ran* are different by only one letter, and *go* and *went* are completely different words.

Practice A Each general word below is followed by a more specific word used in "Jason and the Golden Fleece." On the line, write one more specific word for the general word. **Possible Answers**

1. chair → throne   chair → _____ stool _____

2. said → whispered   said → _____ exclaimed _____

3. clothes → robes   clothes → _____ T-shirts _____

4. monster → dragon   monster → _____ harpy _____

5. entrance → gate   entrance → _____ doorway _____

Practice B   Write the past tense of the following verbs.

6. begin   began

7. choose   chose

8. fly   flew

9. sing   sang

10. teach   taught

Apply

Rewrite the sentences, replacing the underlined words with more specific words that mean the same thing. You will be surprised how much more interesting the sentences will be. **Possible Answers**

11. I decided to read that <u>book</u> because it was about <u>animals</u>.

    I decided to read *Where the Red Fern Grows* because it was about dogs.

12. To get to the <u>building</u>, drive about five miles west on that <u>road</u>.

    To get to the library, drive about five miles west on Highway 12.

13. We watched a <u>performance</u> at the theater, and then went home in a <u>vehicle</u>.

    We watched a dance at the theater, and then went home in a bus.

14. A <u>person</u> yelled at us when we swam out too far in the <u>water</u>.

    A lifeguard yelled at us when we swam out too far in the lake.

Name _____ **Date** _____

Selection Vocabulary

Focus

assassins (ə • sas' • inz) *n.* plural of **assassin:** a person who murders a public figure, such as a government leader (page 614)

challenged (chal' • ənjd) *v.* past tense of **challenge:** call to take part in a contest (page 614)

worthy (wûr' • thē) *adj.* having enough value; deserving (page 614)

throb (throb) *n.* a heavy, fast beat or sensation (page 615)

hideous (hid' • ē • əs) *adj.* extremely ugly; horrible (page 616)

strait (strāt) *n.* a narrow channel between two larger bodies of water (page 617)

destiny (des' • tə • nē) *n.* what happens to a person, especially when it seems to be determined in advance; fortune (page 618)

glistening (glis' • ən • ing) *adj.* shining with reflected light (page 620)

pity (pit' • ē) *n.* a feeling of sorrow and sympathy for the troubles of another (page 620)

gaping (gā' • ping) *adj.* wide open (page 620)

Practice **Write the vocabulary word that best matches the underlined word or phrase in the sentences below.**

1. The wet grass was <u>shining with reflected light</u> soon after the sun rose.

glistening

2. I was <u>called to take part in</u> a basketball game.

challenged

3. The liner sailed through the <u>narrow channel connecting two large bodies of water</u>.

strait

4. Elena had <u>sorrow and sympathy</u> for animals at the shelter.

pity

5. I felt a <u>heavy, fast beat</u> in my thumb after hitting it with the hammer.

throb

6. The agents caught the <u>people who murder a public figure</u> after their plans were discovered.

assassins

7. The <u>extremely ugly</u> painting still hangs in my childhood doctor's office.

hideous

8. To Jenny, the landing area on the aircraft carrier seemed <u>wide open</u>.

gaping

9. At the carnival, the automated, fortune-teller game attempted to tell me <u>what happens to a person, especially when it seems to be determined in advance</u>.

destiny

10. Andrea's speech was <u>having enough value</u> of the praise it received.

worthy

Apply **Match each word on the left to its definition.**

11. hideous

12. glistening

13. destiny

14. gaping

15. strait

a. a narrow channel between two larger bodies of water

b. wide open

c. very ugly; horrible

d. shining with reflected light

e. a feeling of sorrow and sympathy for the troubles of another

f. what happens to a person, especially when it seems to be determined in advance

Name _____ Date _____

Formulating Questions and Problems

A good question or problem to investigate:

Possible Answer What could my classmates or I do to change something about our world?

_____

_____

_____

_____

Why this is an interesting question or problem:

Possible Answer It encourages us to connect the theme Call of Duty to our daily lives. Our impact could be small or it could be enormous. It is empowering.

_____

_____

_____

Some other things I wonder about this question or problem:

Possible Answer How do we convince others that our project is worth supporting?

_____

_____

_____

_____

Formulating Questions and Problems (continued)

My investigation group's question or problem:

Possible Answer What could my classmates or I do to change something about our world? Do we start small and just work to change our classroom, or do we look wider? Can we change our school? Our town? Our country? The world?

_____

_____

What our investigation will contribute to the rest of the class:

Possible Answer Our answers and questions will contribute to the greater class discussion of the topic. We may inspire the class to work on a project together.

_____

_____

_____

Some other things I wonder about this question or problem:

Possible Answer How do we get the community to respect our idea based on its merit rather than give it attention simply because of our youth?

_____

_____

_____

Writing an Invitation

Think

Audience: Who will read your invitation?

Possible Answer my friends from school

Purpose: What is your reason for sending out invitations?

Possible Answer I want to invite my friends to a surprise party for my sister

Prewriting

Invitations provide brief, specific information about what the event is or why it is being held, when it will take place (including the date and time), where it will take place (including the address and sometimes directions) and who is giving the party. Use the organizer below to plan your invitation. Possible Answers

What: A surprise birthday party

Who: Rachel Stinson

When: 6:00–9:00, Saturday, July 22

Where: 5410 Falcon Crest Road

Given By: Amber Summers

Directions: From the school parking lot, turn left (east) onto Broad Street. Continue on Broad Street for six blocks until you see Handyman's Hardware Store on your right. Turn right onto Pine View Avenue and continue heading south for about 2 miles. Turn right on Falcon Crest Road and look to your left for 5410 Falcon Crest. My house is blue with yellow trim. Don't park in the driveway or you'll ruin the surprise!

Now, use a separate piece of paper to create a map to accompany your directions.

Revising
Use this checklist to revise your invitation.

☐ Have you included the details your audience needs to know?

☐ Is your language clear and concise?

☐ Does your invitation provide information about the reason for the event, the time, and the location?

☐ Did you provide clear cardinal and ordinal directions so your recipients can locate the event?

Editing/Proofreading
Use this checklist to make corrections.

☐ Is your invitation formatted correctly?

☐ Did you check all capitalization, spelling, and punctuation?

☐ Have you double-checked your directions and made sure you properly spelled the names of streets and landmarks?

Publishing
Use this checklist to publish your personal letter.

☐ Use spacing and design to enhance the appearance of your invitation.

☐ Neatly rewrite or type your invitation.

Name _____ **Date** _____

Spelling

Focus

- Understanding and identifying **Greek roots** and their meanings can help you define and spell difficult and unfamiliar words. Here are some of the Greek roots in the spelling words and their meanings:

  naut = "ship or sailor"; **cosm** = "universe"; **geo** = "earth"; **ast** = "star"; **meter** or **metry** = "measure"; **graph** = "write"; **therm** = "heat"

- **Irregular verbs** are verbs that do not form the past tense by adding *-ed.*

Word List

1. nautical
2. cosmonaut
3. nautilus
4. astronauts
5. geology
6. geometry
7. geographic
8. geological
9. geometric
10. geothermal
11. understand
12. understood
13. teach
14. taught
15. forgive
16. forgave
17. forgiven
18. break
19. broke
20. broken

Practice

Fill in the appropriate root word and write the resulting spelling word on the line.

1. geo metry   geometry
2. naut ilus   nautilus
3. geo metric   geometric
4. geo graph ic   geographic
5. geo logical   geological
6. astro nauts   astronauts
7. geo therm al   geothermal
8. geo logy   geology
9. cosmo nauts   cosmonaut
10. naut ical   nautical

On the lines, write the present tense and past tense of the irregular verbs.

Possible Answers

Present   Past
11. teach   12. taught
13. understand   14. understood
15. break   16. broke
17. forgive   18. forgave

On the lines, write the two past participles from the spelling list that are forms of the following verbs.

19. break broken   20. forgive forgiven

On the lines, write the spelling words that are represented by the following root and suffix meaning combinations.

21. universe + sailor   cosmonaut
22. earth + logy   geology
23. earth + measurement + ic   geometric
24. star + sailors   astronauts
25. earth + heat + al   geothermal

Select the correctly spelled word in parentheses that completes the sentence, and write it on the line.

26. A (nautilus, nawtilus) is a kind of sea creature.   nautilus
27. A valley is a (gealogical, geological) feature.   geological
28. My sister's favorite subject is (geometry, geomitry)   geometry

Name _____ Date _____

Compound Sentences and Plurals

Focus

A **compound sentence** consists of two or more simple sentences, which are also called independent clauses. The sentences should be connected by a comma and a conjunction, such as *and, or,* or *but,* or a semicolon.

The **plurals** of many words are formed by adding -*s* or -*es.*

- For words that end in a consonant and *y,* change the *y* to *i* and add -*es.*
  cherry, cherries   colony, colonies

- For some words that end in *f* or *fe,* change the *f* or *fe* to *v* and add -*es.*
  wife, wives   calf, calves

- For words that end in a consonant and *o,* you add either -*s* or -*es.*
  piano, pianos   echo, echoes

- For some words, the plural form is a different word.
  woman, women   tooth, teeth

- For some words, the singular and plural forms are the same.
  moose, moose   series, series

Practice A   **Combine each pair of sentences below into a single compound sentence.**

1. Dave wants to see a movie. I want to go skateboarding.
   Dave wants to see a movie, but I want to go skateboarding.

2. Shane met Donetta at the library. They studied together.
   Shane met Donetta at the library, and they studied together.

3. We can make dinner. We can order a pizza.

We can make dinner, or we can order a pizza.

4. Krista trimmed the bushes. Krista raked the leaves.

Krista trimmed the bushes, and she raked the leaves.

5. The bus travels down this street. The street is closed for repairs.

The bus travels down this street, but it is closed for repairs.

Practice B **Write the correct plural form of each singular noun listed below.**

6. leaf   leaves

7. traveler   travelers

8. deer   deer

9. city   cities

10. person   people

 **Apply** **Place a check mark next to each sentence that is a compound sentence and an X next to each simple sentence. Then add the missing commas to the compound sentences.**

11. ____✓____ My friend and I built a model airplane, and we displayed it at school.

12. ____X____ Our teacher was impressed with our finished product.

13. ____✓____ Mr. Jefferson had flown the same kind of plane in the Air Force, and he told us about his experiences.

14. ____X____ Paul always knew he would become a teacher or a pilot for an airline.

15. ____X____ He loves sharing his knowledge with others.

Name _____ **Date** _____

Irregular Plurals and Base Word Families

> **Focus** The plurals of many words are formed by adding *-s* or *-es*.
> **Irregular plurals** do not follow this rule.
>
> • For some words, the plural form is a different word.
>   man, men   foot, feet
>
> • For some words, the singular and plural forms are the same.
>   trout, trout   deer, deer
>
> A **base word** is a word that can stand alone when all prefixes,
> suffixes, and inflected endings are removed. Identifying and
> understanding base words can help you define difficult and
> unfamiliar words.

Practice A

For each singular word below, write its plural form on the line.

1. species ___ species ___
2. series ___ series ___
3. sheep ___ sheep ___
4. person ___ people ___
5. tooth ___ teeth ___

6. mouse ___ mice ___
7. moose ___ moose ___
8. woman ___ women ___
9. goose ___ geese ___
10. foot ___ feet ___

Practice B

Identify the common base word in the words below.

11. historical, historian, prehistoric ___ history ___
12. understanding, misunderstanding, understandable ___ understand ___
13. acceptable, acceptance, accepted ___ accept ___
14. agreement, disagree, agreeable ___ agree ___
15. uncover, coverage, discover ___ cover ___

Apply Read the following sentences. If the sentence contains a correct plural form, place a check mark on the line. If the plural form is incorrect, rewrite the sentence using the correct form. Use a dictionary if you need help.

16. _____ We love to watch the salmons swim in the stream.

We love to watch the salmon swim in the stream.

17. _____ Several of the mans on the field ran to help the dog.

Several of the men on the field ran to help the dog.

18. ___✓___ We caught eight fish last time we went to that particular lake.

_____

_____

19. _____ Many of the pioneers used oxes to pull their wagons west.

Many of the pioneers used oxen to pull their wagons west.

20. _____ Both childs love to study dinosaurs.

Both children love to study dinosaurs.

Name _____ Date _____

Selection Vocabulary

Focus

sport (sport) *n.* amusement; fun (page 630)

descended (di • send' • əd) *v.* past tense of **descend:** to come down (page 630)

quest (kwest) *n.* a search or pursuit (page 631)

beaded (bēd' • əd) *adj.* covered with drops (page 631)

task (task) *n.* a piece of work to be done (page 632)

lumbered (lum' • bərd) *v.* past tense of **lumber:** to move about in a clumsy, noisy way (page 633)

exhausted (ig • zost' • əd) *adj.* weak or tired (page 634)

loyalty (loi' • əl • tē) *n.* strong and lasting affection and support; allegiance (page 635)

spring (spring) *adj.* from a place where underground water comes out of the earth (page 636)

fitter (fit' • ər) *adj.* healthier; in better physical shape (page 637)

Practice   Write the vocabulary word next to the group of words that have a similar meaning.

1. faithfulness; trustworthiness _____ loyalty _____

2. chore; job _____ task _____

3. journey; search _____ quest _____

4. wet with dew; covered in droplets _____ beaded _____

5. well; fountain _____ spring _____

6. fell; plummeted _____ descended _____

7. plodded; stumbled _____ lumbered _____

8. healthier; more robust _____ fitter _____

9. recreation; amusement _____ sport _____

10. emptied; depleted _____ exhausted _____

Apply Write the selection vocabulary word that best answers each question below.

11. If Reggie exercises for half an hour each day, what will he become?

fitter

12. Which word describes snow that has fallen to the ground?

descended

13. Which word describes prospectors searching for gold?

quest

14. What does the outside of a glass of ice water become on a hot day?

beaded

15. Hot water bubbling out of the ground is an example of what?

spring

16. Which word describes how a cow might have walked over uneven ground?

lumbered

Name _____ Date _____

Making Conjectures

Our question or problem:

Possible Answer What types of careers exist for someone

who wants to help people?

_____

_____

_____

_____

Conjecture (my first theory or explanation):

Possible Answer I think becoming a firefighter is a good

career for someone who wants to help people.

_____

_____

_____

_____

_____

_____

_____

As you collect information, your conjecture will change. Return to this page to record your new theories or explanations about your question or problem.

Establishing Investigation Needs

My group's question or problem:

Possible Answer What types of careers exist for someone
who wants to help people?

Knowledge Needs—Information I need to find or figure out in
order to investigate the question or problem:

A. **Possible Answer** I need to do research on how firefighters perform their jobs.

B. **Possible Answer** What kind of people choose to become firefighters?

C. **Possible Answer** What is rewarding about the job?

D. _____

E. _____

Source	Useful?	How?
Encyclopedias		
Books		
Magazines		
Newspapers		
Video and audio clips		
Television		
Interviews, observations	yes	to get a firefighter's perspective
Museums	yes	to learn about firefighters
Other:	yes	for graphics about job training

Name _____ Date _____

Play Sketch, Week 1

Think **Audience: Who** will read your play? **Possible Answers**

my classmates

Purpose: What is your reason for writing a play?

I want to entertain my audience.

Prewriting Although the format for a play looks different
from other writing, the plot still has the
same structure as other forms of literature. Use the following
graphic organizer to plan your play. **Possible Answers**

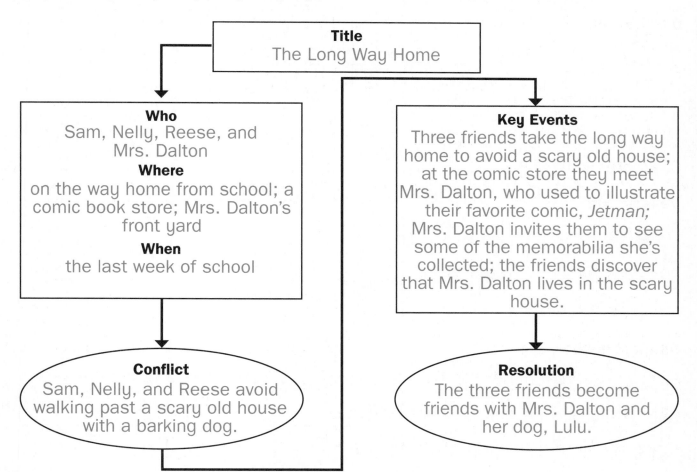

Title
The Long Way Home

Who
Sam, Nelly, Reese, and
Mrs. Dalton
Where
on the way home from school; a
comic book store; Mrs. Dalton's
front yard
When
the last week of school

Key Events
Three friends take the long way
home to avoid a scary old house;
at the comic store they meet
Mrs. Dalton, who used to illustrate
their favorite comic, *Jetman*;
Mrs. Dalton invites them to see
some of the memorabilia she's
collected; the friends discover
that Mrs. Dalton lives in the scary
house.

Conflict
Sam, Nelly, and Reese avoid
walking past a scary old house
with a barking dog.

Resolution
The three friends become
friends with Mrs. Dalton and
her dog, Lulu.

Drafting Use the lines below to create character sketches with your group for each of the main characters in your play. You may describe the way your characters look, feel, think, and act. You do not have to write in complete sentences. Use your sketches to help you as you draft your play. **Possible Answers**

Character #1: Sam

Description: tall, skinny, with freckles

awkward and shy, looks at the floor when he's

nervous

Character #2: Nelly

Description: Small and tough, loud and talkative

likes to do daring things

is known for boasting and making up stories

Character #3: Reese

Description: Smart and outgoing, caring friend

Really likes comic books

Makes a lot of jokes

Character #4: Mrs. Dalton

Description: Middle aged woman, odd clothes, blue eyes

Intelligent, uses big words

Very friendly even though she is scary at first

Name _____ Date _____

Spelling

Focus

- A **base word family** is a family of words that share a base word. A base word can take many different forms when different prefixes, suffixes, and roots are added.

- The suffix **-ness** means "the state or quality of" or "capable or worthy of."

Practice Add the suffix **-ness** to the following base words.

1. sluggish — sluggishness
2. willing — willingness
3. happy — happiness
4. wicked — wickedness
5. selfish — selfishness
6. stiff — stiffness
7. timely — timeliness
8. coarse — coarseness
9. lazy — laziness
10. tired — tiredness

Word List

1. happiness
2. tiredness
3. timeliness
4. wickedness
5. coarseness
6. willingness
7. stiffness
8. sluggishness
9. laziness
10. selfishness
11. colony
12. colonial
13. colonist
14. colonization
15. company
16. companion
17. accompany
18. carried
19. carriage
20. carrier

For each word in the family, select the correct form of the base word to form the whole spelling word.

Base word: colony

11. _____zation — colonization
12. _____ist — colonist
13. _____ial — colonial

Base word: company

14. _____on   companion

15. ac_____   accompany

Base word: carry

16. _____er   carrier

17. _____ed   carried

18. _____age   carriage

Apply On the line, write the spelling word that is related to each of the following words.

19. sluggishly   sluggishness

20. lazy   laziness

21. time   timeliness

22. unhappy   happiness

23. timeless   timeliness

In the following sentences, correct each underlined word and write it on the line. If the word is already correct, write *correct.*

24. The <u>kolony</u> in the New World grew slowly at first.   colony

25. My dog is a good <u>cumpanion</u>.   companion

26. Will we ever see the <u>colunization</u> of the moon?   colonization

27. My father works for a large <u>company</u>.   correct

28. We <u>caried</u> our books to the library.   carried

Name _____ **Date** _____

Prepositions, Prepositional Phrases, and Apostrophes

- A **prepositional phrase** is a group of words that begins with a preposition and ends with the object of the preposition.

- A **preposition** shows the relationship between the main word in the phrase and another word in the sentence.
  He visited the house **near** the river.

Apostrophes are used to show possession.

- For most singular nouns, add 's.
  cat's ears, boss's necktie

- For plural nouns that end with s, add an apostrophe.
  flowers' petals, troops' uniforms

- For singular proper nouns that end in s, always add 's.
  Harris's backyard, Chris's haircut

A contraction is formed by combining two words and omitting one or more letters. The **apostrophe** replaces the missing letters.
  do not, don't   we will, we'll   you have, you've

Practice A   Underline the prepositional phrase(s) in each sentence.

1. Yao always took the same path to school.

2. Darren enjoyed visiting the animal shelter near the school.

3. Hannah enjoyed playing with her puppy until it was time for work.

4. After the game, Nitesh raced home to watch the news.

5. After his exercise routine, Gary always made sure to drink plenty of water.

Practice B — Insert apostrophes where they are needed in the following sentences.

6. I'm on my way to the Harris's annual barbecue.

7. This year they're going to borrow the Cohens' croquet set for the day.

8. In the past, we've used our next-door neighbors' volleyball net, but they had moved away recently.

9. We're bringing our family's folding chairs like we've done for every cookout.

10. I'll call you later tonight, and we'll discuss the day's events.

Apply — Create a prepositional phrase, and write it on the line using the preposition in parentheses. Use the phrase in an original sentence.

Answers will vary.

11. (under) _____

_____

12. (from) _____

_____

13. (beside) _____

_____

14. (against) _____

_____

15. (above) _____

_____

Name _____ **Date** _____

Possessives and the Prefix *pre-*

Practice A Change each singular possessive below into a plural possessive.

	Singular	Plural	
1.	messenger's drum	messengers'	drums
2.	boy's bow and arrow	boys'	bows and arrows
3.	woman's stick	women's	sticks
4.	tiger's neck	tigers'	necks
5.	princess's eyes	princesses'	eyes
6.	contest's winner	contests'	winners
7.	child's honesty	children's	honesty
8.	wife's veil	wives'	veils
9.	necklace's stones	necklaces'	stones
10.	brave's gift	braves'	gifts

Practice B   Add the prefix *pre-* to the following words, and then use each new word in a sentence.

Possible Answers

11. planned   preplanned

Our trip to the store was preplanned so we would not

forget anything.

12. heat   preheat

You will need to preheat the oven before starting the

recipe.

13. treat   pre-treat

We had to pre-treat the dirty clothes before putting them

in the washing machine.

14. approval   pre-approval

Students need pre-approval before they can take part in

after-school activities.

15. washed   prewashed

The lettuce in that bag has been prewashed.

Apply   On a separate sheet of paper, use five of the plural possessives from the previous section in original sentences. In each sentences include one word with the prefix *pre-*. **Answers will vary.**

Name _____ Date _____

Selection Vocabulary

Focus

Paraguay (par' • ə • gwā') *n.* a country in central South America (page 646)

murals (myo͞or' • əlz) *n.* plural of **mural:** a picture that is painted on a wall. A mural usually covers most of a wall. (page 646)

irritably (ir' • i • tə • blē) *adv.* in an angry or impatient way (page 647)

pleading (plē' • ding) *v.* making a sincere request; begging (page 647)

burdened (bûr' • dend) *adj.* weighed down with a heavy load (page 648)

noble (nō' • bəl) *adj.* having greatness of inner nature (page 652)

scowls (skoulz) *v.* frowns in an angry way (page 655)

rare (râr) *adj.* not often found (page 659)

intricate (in' • tri • kit) *adj.* involved or complicated, complex (page 660)

murmur (mûr' • mûr) *v.* to make or say with a low, soft sound (page 662)

Practice Choose the word that matches each definition below, and write it on the line.

1. _____intricate_____ complicated; complex
2. _____burdened_____ weighed down
3. _____pleading_____ begging
4. _____noble_____ having inner greatness
5. _____murmur_____ speak softly
6. _____murals_____ wall paintings

7. _____ irritably _____ impatiently

8. _____ Paraguay _____ South American country

9. _____ rare _____ not often found

10. _____ scowls _____ frowns

Apply **Fill in each blank with the selection vocabulary word that best completes the sentence.**

11. Isabel was _____ pleading _____ with her coach to be put into the game.

12. After years of searching, the biologist found a _____ rare _____ species of butterfly.

13. Some of our downtown buildings have colorful _____ murals _____ painted on them.

14. Ideally, only _____ noble _____ people would take part in politics.

15. My sister _____ scowls _____ every time I beat her at checkers.

Name _____ **Date** _____

Play Sketch: Week 2

Possible Answers

**Think**

Audience: For whom will you perform your play?

<u>my teacher</u>

Purpose: What do you want your performance to accomplish?

<u>I want it tell an interesting story.</u>

**Revising**

Use the graphic organizer below to make sure your play has a beginning, a middle, and an ending.

Beginning: <u>Sam, Nelly, and Reese take the long way home from school to avoid a scary old house. They talk about the house and the barking dog that makes them nervous.</u>

Middle: <u>At the comic store, the three friends meet Mrs. Dalton. They are excited to learn that she once illustrated their favorite comic. She invites them to her home.</u>

Ending: <u>The three friends meet the barking dog, Lulu, and learn that she is friendly. They become good friends with Mrs. Dalton.</u>

Revising
Use this checklist to revise your play.

☐ Do the opening lines grab your audience's attention?

☐ Are your characters believable and well-rounded?

☐ Is your dialogue natural and realistic and appropriate for each character?

☐ Is the dialogue written at a level your audience will understand and enjoy?

☐ Do your dialogue and stage directions clearly describe the setting and show what happens?

Editing/Proofreading
Use this checklist to correct mistakes.

☐ Have you used the standard formatting for a play including dialogue and stage directions?

☐ Have you spelled the names of people and places consistently and capitalized proper nouns?

☐ Do your subjects and verbs agree?

☐ Have you checked that all dependent clauses are joined to an independent clause by a comma?

Publishing
Use this checklist to publish your play.

☐ Choose students to act out the roles in your play, and practice your performance.

☐ Perform your play for the class.

Name _____ **Date** _____

Spelling

Focus
- The prefix *pre-* means "before." It can be added to a word that begins with a consonant or vowel.
- **Multiple-meaning words** are words with more than one meaning but the same word origins.

Practice On the line, write the spelling word that results when the prefix *pre-* is added to the word parts.

1. cooked   precooked
2. judge   prejudge
3. caution   precaution
4. load   preload
5. determine   predetermine
6. occupied   preoccupied
7. mature   premature
8. order   preorder
9. arrange   prearrange
10. historic   prehistoric

On the line, write the spelling word that corresponds with the following pairs of definitions.

11. "to move or struggle" and "a kind of fish"   flounder

12. "certain" and "greater than zero"   positive

Word List
1. prearrange
2. precaution
3. premature
4. preoccupied
5. prehistoric
6. prejudge
7. preload
8. preorder
9. precooked
10. predetermine
11. flounder
12. disposal
13. refrain
14. positive
15. manual
16. residency
17. general
18. resort
19. flourish
20. ground

13. "to grow strongly or thrive" and "to wave about boldly"

14. "earth or land" and "did grind"

15. "common or affecting everyone" and "a military officer"

16. "use for help" or "place for recreation"

17. "to hold oneself back" or "a phrase or verse in a song"

18. "throwing away" or "the act of settling something"

19. "relating to or done by hands" or "instruction book"

20. "place one lives" or "training for a doctor"

flourish
ground

general
resort
refrain
disposal
manual
residency

 **Apply**   **Match the appropriate spelling word to the phrase that best describes it.**

21. worried

22. determine beforehand

23. load in advance

24. arrange beforehand

25. order in advance

preoccupied
predetermine
preload
prearrange
preorder

Use context clues to determine the meaning of the underlined word and write it on the line. Use the definitions given on the previous page.

26. Do you know the <u>refrain</u> of that song?
a phrase or verse in a song or poem that is repeated

27. I like <u>flounder</u> better than trout.
kind of fish

28. The plants will <u>flourish</u> with all this sunlight.
to grow strongly or thrive

Name _____ **Date** _____

Complex Sentences, Independent and Dependent Clauses

Focus

- A **complex sentence** contains an independent clause and one or more dependent clauses.

- An **independent clause** stands alone as a sentence.

- A **dependent clause** has a subject and a verb, but it cannot stand alone as a sentence.

- **Dependent clauses** modify words in sentences. They are used as either adjectives or adverbs.

- I found the book in the fiction section.

- I found the book **that Julie needed for school** in the fiction section.

- *That Julie needed for school* modifies the noun *book*, so it is being used as an adjective.

Practice A Label each sentence with *C* if it is a complex sentence or *X* if it is not a complex sentence.

1. __C__ After Aziza finishes working on the computer, she logs out before turning off the power.

2. __X__ The lights dimmed as the movie started, and everyone in the theater became silent.

3. __C__ Maya's uncle, who visits a couple of times a year, always brings news about friends and relatives who still live in Dallas.

4. __X__ The sheriff told the posse to head out while the sun still shone, and then he walked back inside the building.

5. __C__ After Paul finished writing the novel, he got his book published.

Practice B   Underline the independent clause, and circle the
dependent clause in each sentence.

6. (After Jim's mom dropped us off,) we headed to English class.

7. (As the bus was pulling away,) Jeremy ran out of his house to the bus stop.

8. (Since the Shamrocks won the softball game,) the entire town had a big
celebration.

9. The dog always ran away after dinner, (because he knew he was getting a
bath).

10. Matt always got up early during the summer, (because sometimes his
grandfather would let him ride the tractor.)

Apply   On a separate sheet of paper, combine each set of
clauses below to create a complex sentence. Be sure
to use one or more of the conjunctions, relative pronouns, and
subordinating conjunctions from the box.   Answers will vary.

when	and	that	whenever
unless	than	because	so
after			

11. it's cold enough; my friend Donyell ice skates

12. Angelo studied at the library yesterday; it was much quieter

13. a special visitor was coming for dinner; I helped clean the house

14. Krista finds the map; she won't know the way to the reunion

15. they had sprayed with water; the fire fighters left; smoke continued to rise
from the building

Name _____ Date _____

Homophones and Word Relationships

Homophones are words that sound the same but have different spellings and meanings.

The following word pair is an example of a homophone: *would* and *wood*.

Identifying and understanding **word relationships** can give you clues about the meanings of difficult and unfamiliar words.

Practice A The underlined word in each sentence is half of a homophone pair. Write the other half on the line followed by its definition.

1. "Sometimes <u>our</u> guests bring little gifts."

_____hour_____ Definition: <u>sixty minutes</u>

2. "She was used to getting her <u>way</u>."

_____weigh_____ Definition: <u>discover how heavy something is</u>

3. "She cut a <u>piece</u>, wrapped it in a cloth napkin, and brought it upstairs . . ."

_____peace_____ Definition: <u>nonviolence or the opposite of war</u>

4. "Helen <u>ate</u> the cake very quickly . . ."

_____eight_____ Definition: <u>the number between seven and nine</u>

5. "The two weeks in the garden house <u>passed</u> quickly . . ."

_____past_____ Definition: <u>what happened before the present</u>

Practice B — Identify how each word group is related, and write it on the line.

6. treadmill, jump rope, weights, medicine ball

   exercise equipment

7. green beans, corn, spinach, carrots

   types of vegetables

8. quatrain, lyric, free verse

   types of poetry

9. expository text, historical fiction, biography, realistic fiction

   literary genres

10. drums, xylophone, tuba, saxophone

    types of musical instruments

Apply — Circle the homophone that correctly completes each sentence below.

11. It has been nearly a (weak, (week)) since the last snowstorm.

12. Will (their, (there)) be cake and ice cream at the party?

13. The tables at the park are made of (steal, (steel)).

14. Take a ((peek), peak) at this note I am giving to Sydney.

15. Shawn looked (threw, (through)) the newspaper for coupons.

Name _____ Date _____

Selection Vocabulary

Focus

soiled (soild) *v.* past tense of **soil:** to make or become dirty (page 674)

lunged (lunjd) *v.* past tense of **lunge:** to move forward suddenly (page 675)

distract (dis • trakt') *v.* to draw one's attention away from what one is doing or thinking (page 675)

amusing (ə • mū' • zing) *adj.* entertaining (page 675)

imitating (i' • mi • tāt' • ing) *v.* acting just as another person does; copying (page 675)

sulking (sulk' • ing) *v.* acting angry and silent (page 676)

aromas (ə • rō' • məs) *n.* plural of **aroma:** a pleasant or agreeable smell (page 677)

remark (ri • märk') *n.* a short statement or comment (page 677)

disturbed (dis • tûrbd') *adj.* upset or confused (page 678)

insistently (in • sis' • tənt • lē) *adv.* in a strong or firm manner (page 678)

Practice **Write the word that best completes each sentence.**

1. Casey was _imitating_ Mrs. Ito when she suddenly walked into the room.
2. The fair was filled with the _aromas_ of cotton candy and fried food.
3. Antoine misheard the principal's _remark_ and thought he was in trouble.
4. I was _disturbed_ by an accident I saw on the freeway.
5. The mud on the bottom of my shoes _soiled_ the rug.
6. Everyone found the playful puppies to be quite _amusing_.
7. I was thrown back into my seat when the taxi _lunged_ forward.
8. I tried to _distract_ my parents, while my sister bought their birthday presents.
9. After his team had lost the game, Jim would not stop _sulking_.
10. Because it was almost time for the bank to close, Andy _insistently_ requested the location of the bank.

Apply Place a check mark next to the correct example for each selection vocabulary word.

1. Which is an example of something **amusing?**

   ✓ a clown juggling at a circus   _____ a car waiting at a stoplight

2. Which is an example of someone making a **remark?**

   ✓ a teacher praising your work   _____ a friend laughing at a joke

3. Which is an example of **imitating?**

   ✓ copying the way an actor speaks   _____ wearing a suit and tie

4. Which is an example of being **disturbed?**

   _____ dropping your notebook   ✓ realizing you are lost

5. Which is an example of something that is **soiled?**

   ✓ T-shirt with pizza sauce on it   _____ house that needs paint

Name _____ **Date** _____

Making Inferences

Writers often do not include every detail about a character or an event in the story. Readers must use clues from the text to make inferences in order to complete the picture. **Making inferences** means using the writer's clues, and your own prior knowledge and experiences, to gain a better understanding of the character or event.

Practice Find two sentences in the selection from which you can infer something about Annie's character. Write the page numbers and sentences below. Then write a phrase telling the inference you made about Annie's character from the sentence. **Possible Answers**

1. Page: _____679_____

Sentence: _"'I spell into her hand everything we do all day long, although she has no idea yet what the spelling means,' Annie wrote."_

What the reader can infer about Annie from this sentence:
Annie is patient and dedicated.

2. Page: _____675_____

Sentence: _"Annie pulled out a watch to distract Helen, who was beginning to get flushed and make angry sounds because she could not have the bag."_

What the reader can infer about Annie from this sentence:
Annie is quick-thinking.

Apply Use your prior knowledge to make inferences based on each of the following sentences. Possible Answers

Example:

You look out the window and see people wearing heavy coats, hats, and gloves.

Inference: _It is cold outside._

3. You hear pots and pans banging in the kitchen, and you start to smell something good.

Inference: Something is cooking.

4. Fred didn't feel good yesterday, and he is not at school today.

Inference: Fred stayed home sick.

5. Every time Susan goes to Ted's house, his cat jumps into her lap and purrs.

Inference: Ted's cat likes Susan.

6. The dog gobbles up the beef treats you give him but spits out the chicken ones. The dog does not like the

Inference: chicken treats.

Name _____ Date _____

Writing a Realistic Story

Think

Audience: Who will read your realistic story? **Possible Answers**
my classmates

Purpose: What do you want your readers to think about your story?
I want my readers to think my
dialogue sounds realistic.

Prewriting One of the most basic rules that good writers follow is
"show; don't tell." Using the lines below write a sentence
describing part of the character's personality or an emotion. Then, write one
or two sentences showing the character demonstrating this characteristic.
Possible Answers

Character 1

Telling: Michelle is bossy.

Showing: Michelle came into the classroom and
ordered her friend Tyson out of his chair. She
needed it to hang a poster on the wall.

Character 2

Telling: Tyson is angry.

Showing: Tyson sat with his arms folded and a
frown on his face. His ears were slowly turning
red.

Revising
Use this checklist to begin revising your draft.

☐ Have you developed your characters enough? Are they believable?

☐ Does your story have a believable conflict, rising action, climax, and resolution?

☐ Did you write realistic dialogue for each character?

☐ Are the settings in your story vivid and believable?

☐ Did you delete irrelevant or repetitive ideas and consolidate similar ideas?

Editing/Proofreading
Use this checklist to begin editing your draft.

☐ Are the names you have invented for people and places realistic?

☐ Have you spelled the names of people and places consistently throughout your story?

☐ Do the key events of your story happen in a logical order?

☐ Did you check for correct, consistent verb tense and correct any misused words?

Publishing
Use this checklist to prepare for your next draft.

☐ Neatly retype or rewrite your story and include any illustrations.

☐ Place your story in your Writing Portfolio so you can evaluate your growth.

Name _____ Date _____

Spelling

Focus
Understanding and identifying **Latin roots** and their meanings can help you define and spell difficult and unfamiliar words. Here are some of the Latin roots in the spelling words and their meanings:

anim = "life, spirit"; ***spec*** = "see"; ***mob*** = "move"; ***rupt*** = "break"

Practice Fill in the appropriate Latin root and write the spelling word.

1. in**anim**ate   inanimate
2. **spec**tacle   spectacle
3. auto**mob**ile   automobile
4. **rupt**ure   rupture
5. inter**rupt**   interrupt
6. **spec**ulate   speculate
7. in**spec**t   inspect
8. **mob**ilize   mobilize
9. **anim**ation   animation
10. bank**rupt**   bankrupt
11. e**rupt**   erupt
12. ex**pec**t   expect
13. ab**rupt**   abrupt
14. **spec**tator   spectator
15. **mob**ility   mobility

Word List
1. animate
2. animal
3. animation
4. inanimate
5. animosity
6. inspect
7. spectacle
8. spectator
9. speculate
10. expect
11. mobile
12. automobile
13. mobility
14. mobilize
15. immobile
16. rupture
17. erupt
18. bankrupt
19. abrupt
20. interrupt

16. <u>mob</u>ile   mobile
17. <u>anim</u>ate   animate
18. <u>anim</u>osity   animosity
19. im<u>mob</u>ile   immobile
20. <u>anim</u>al   animal

Apply **Decide which Latin root correctly completes the word in each sentence. Write the spelling word.**

21. Please do not inter<u>rupt</u> when someone is speaking.

22. They were im<u>mob</u>ile with fear.

23. A rock is an in<u>anim</u>ate object.

24. We tried to <u>anim</u>ate the tired group.

25. We ex<u>pec</u>t to get a lot of rain this week.

26. There was a <u>rupt</u>ure in his thigh muscle.

27. Do not make a <u>spec</u>tacle of yourself.

28. You can sense the <u>anim</u>osity between the cat and the dog.

29. Our auto<u>mob</u>ile is stopped at the light.

30. That volcano may e<u>rupt</u> at any minute.

interrupt
immobile
inanimate
animate
expect
rupture
spectacle

animosity
automobile
erupt

If the underlined spelling word is misspelled, correct it. If the word is already correct, write *correct*.

31. My favorite <u>anamal</u> is a horse.

32. The troops began to <u>mobalize</u>.

33. The company finally went <u>bankrupped</u>.

34. They <u>inspecked</u> all of the suitcases.

35. Is that an old <u>mobile</u> phone?

animal
mobilize
bankrupt
inspect
correct

Modifiers, Pronouns, Misused Verbs, and Appositives

Focus

- An important part of writing well is being able to recognize misused words. By carefully rereading what you have written and listening closely to how each word is used, you can spot verbs, pronouns, and modifiers that have been used incorrectly.

- An **appositive** is a noun that modifies or renames another noun or pronoun.

  My school, **DuBois Elementary,** is a fun place to learn.

- An **appositive phrase** is an appositive and the words that modify it.

  Uncle Chris went to France, **a country in Europe,** to study art.

Practice A Circle the verb that correctly completes each sentence below.

1. Yesterday my brother and I (road, rode) the bus downtown to the library.

2. It (was, were) the first time I ever traveled on the bus without my mom.

3. We (set, sat) near the front of the bus in the last available seats.

4. At the library, my brother (learned, taught) me how to search for a book using the computer.

5. We (look, looked) in three different sections before finally locating the book.

Underline the appositive or appositive phrase in each sentence. If there is no appositive in the sentence, write an *X* on the line.

6. _____ My youngest brother, <u>T. J.</u>, collects baseball cards.

7. _____ Rollie, <u>the oldest brother</u>, was idolized by all the younger kids in the neighborhood.

8. _X_ The baseball glove in the window was not for sale.

9. _____ My oldest sister, <u>Francesca Leon</u>, is a marine biologist.

10. _____ The spinner dolphin, <u>a type of dolphin that rotates in the air</u>, jumps high out of the water and spins up to 14 times before landing.

Apply The sentences below contains numerous misused words. Read each sentence carefully, and then rewrite it correctly on the lines that follow.

11. Lonnie think its more fun to skateboard then it is to ride a bike.

Lonnie thinks it's more fun to skateboard than it is to ride a bike.

_____

_____

12. When I rose my hand, the teacher says, "You can make one more comment, but than we need to move on."

When I raised my hand, the teacher said, "You may make one more comment, but then we need to move on."

Grammar, Usage, and Mechanics • *Skills Practice 2*